The CAGE & AVIARY BIRD
H A N D B O O K

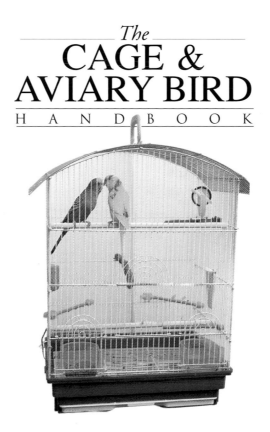

The
CAGE &
AVIARY BIRD
H A N D B O O K

Tony Tilford

NEW
HOLLAND

This paperback edition first published in 2001
by New Holland Publishers (UK) Ltd
London • Cape Town • Sydney • Auckland

Garfield House	80 McKenzie	14 Aquatic Drive	218 Lake Road
86 Edgware Road	Street	Frenchs Forest	Northcote
W2 2EA	Cape Town 8001	NSW 2086	Auckland
United Kingdom	South Africa	Australia	New Zealand

ISBN   1 85974 189 4 (hardback)
       1 85974 237 8 (paperback)

Designer: Lyndall du Toit
Editor: Gail Jennings
Project Manager: Claudia dos Santos
Publisher: Mariëlle Renssen
Illustrator: Steven Felmore
Consultant: Bob Watts (UK) and Dr John Cooke (USA)
Indexer and Proofreader: Inge du Plessis

Reproduction by Unifoto (Pty) Ltd
Printed and bound in Singapore by Tien Wah Press (Pte) Ltd

10 9 8 7 6 5 4 3

Author's Acknowledgements
This book would not have been possible without
generous help from friends throughout the world.
I am therefore sincerely grateful to them all, especially my son, Robert, and John and Joyce Cooke,
along with John Goldsmith and Roy and Gail
Edmonds, whose support has been munificent.

Mentioning everyone who has generously assisted
within the constraints of space is impossible. However,
my thanks go out to all, especially Edi Swoboda and

I Putu Sidartha, along with the staff of the Bali Bird Park, particularly Jiri Holba, Wawan and Dr Maryke. Also from Bali – Bayu, Adi, Ketut and Eka, and Mr Siswanto and family. And not forgetting Dolores Noonan, Phil Warne, Geoff Smith, Raymond Sawyer, Tony and Millie Tugman, Mr and Mrs Moyser, Ivor Grogan, Peter Scott, Roger Millstead, Tony Joliffe, Geoff Walker and Dr Stefan Koudis, Vic, John and Andrew Cole, The Midland Roller Canary Club and The British Budgerigar Society.

Publishers' Acknowledgements
The publishers would like to thank Walter Mangold, Jane Goodfellow, Hendrik Louw and Claire Peché of the World of Birds in Hout Bay, South Africa, for information and access to the birds in the park.

PAGE TWO *Yellow-billed Hornbill* (Tockus flavirostris)
PAGE THREE *Pied Barbet* (Lybius leucomelas)
PAGE FIVE *Violaceous Turaco* (Musophaga violacea)
PAGE SIX *Yellow and Blue Macaws* (Ara ararauna)

CONTENTS

THE NATURE OF BIRDS

A BRIEF HISTORY OF BIRD-KEEPING

People have always had a close association with birds – that much is clear from the numerous representations of birds in ancient art. The nature of these early relationships, however, is not clear. Most of the cave paintings of the Upper Palaeolithic period some 15,000 years ago appear to have had quasi-religious significance, intended to ensure success in the hunt rather than depict pet-keeping for pleasure.

The ancient Egyptians provide the first clear evidence of birds as pets, where in many tomb paintings doves and parrots appear as household pets – these scenes were usually based upon the artist's own experience.

Many early Egyptians believed that in the afterlife, the human spirit survived in the form of a bird. A dead person would remain in the tomb all night, but might visit the living during the day in the shape of Ba, a winged spirit.

The more wealthy Egyptians kept hawks for sport and to capture food for the table, while records dating back some 2,000 years suggest that wild birds were kept for sport in China, too.

The Old Testament texts tell of snaring, fowling and caging, indicating that birds were captured for pleasure and profit many thousands of years ago. Some of the earliest known legislation enacted to protect birds is found in the Old Testament book of Deuteronomy, which prohibits the taking of birds with young.

Likewise, Alexander the Great, King of Macedon (356–323 BC), banned the capture of peacocks for food, because of their beauty.

The Alexandrine Parakeet.

ABOVE *Birds form the decoration of this painted mask from Bali.*
TOP *Anna's Hummingbird (Calypte anna) in flight.*
PREVIOUS PAGES *Throughout the history of art, birds are frequently used to evoke a mystical, earthly paradise.*

The Barn Swallow (Hirundo rustica) *is remarkably agile in the air while catching insects, and makes long-distance migratory flights exploiting any available food sources.*

Alexander the Great also figures in the history of bird-keeping for other reasons. Upon his successful invasion of northern India in 327BC, after having crossed the Indus River the year before, one of his generals presented him with a local pet bird, a large green parakeet, today known as the Alexandrine Parakeet (*Psittacula eupatria*). It is also claimed that Alexander's warriors were often accompanied by their birds as they marched into battle.

Bird-keeping was as popular in ancient Greece as it is today, where dealers specialized in breeding as well as selling birds. Peacocks, highly prized for their plumage, were the most valued, while finches provided the bulk of the business. Jackdaws, their wings clipped to prevent escape, were also favoured and enjoyed relative freedom within courtyard gardens.

Another bird treasured by the Greeks was the Greater Hill Mynah (*Gracula religiosa*); in India the mynah was considered so sacred that, on feast days, individual birds would be paraded on the backs of oxen. The mynah's attraction, then as now, lies in its remarkable ability to imitate the human voice, a skill

*The Jackdaw (*Corvus monedula*) frequently lives close to humans.*

11

also possessed by many parrots. (The earliest report of talking parrots, based on the hearsay accounts of Indian merchants, dates from the Persian Achaemenid dynasty in the early 5th century BC.)

The ancient Egyptians exalted the Sacred Ibis (*Threskiornis aethipica*), while the Hoopoe (*Upupa epops*) was revered in India.

The Hoopoe also features in the famous Classical Greek comedy by Aristophanes, called *Birds*. In the play, about a mythical hero who was turned into a bird, a long lyric poem is sung by the Hoopoe character. He calls all the other birds to a meeting, using the kind of bird-mimicry used by the ancient Greek bird-snarers.

The first aviaries were built by the Romans, who called them 'ornithones'. Their primary purpose was to fatten birds for the table; the birds were fed chiefly on figs that had been chewed to a pulp by special slaves kept for that purpose. To prevent the captive birds from pining as a result of seeing their free companions, they were kept fully enclosed. Clearly the scale of such aviaries was substantial, for the Roman general Sulla (138–78BC) records one such establishment that supplied 5,000 thrushes a year. The Romans also valued birds for the beauty of their song, though to prevent escape the songsters were usually blinded. In addition, this cruel practice ensured that the birds sang throughout the day, mistaking their twilight world for the faint light of dawn – the time they would naturally be most vocal. Parrots were 'trained' in the same way. According to Pliny the Elder, a Roman traveller writing in the 1st century, parrots were kept in near darkness in the belief that they would learn to 'talk' much more quickly if left undistracted.

Throughout Europe are many ancient dovecotes, reminders that pigeons and doves played an important role in the diets of early Europeans, too. Birds were not kept only as food and for song, though. The Roman military used carrier pigeons to transmit important messages (a practice that was still in use during World War II).

In medieval Europe, exotic pets and birds were status symbols and therefore the privilege of royalty and the very wealthy. In 1493 Columbus returned from the New World with a pair of Cuban Amazon Parrots (*Amazona leucocephala*) as a gift for his patron, Queen Isabella of Spain.

Little is known of bird-keeping in the New World, although birds such as the Resplendent Quetzal (*Pharomachrus mocinno*) were long regarded as sacred in the Mayan and Aztec empires. The recent exploration of limestone caves in the extreme southeastern corner of the Dominican Republic has yielded new information about the Taina people, early victims of Columbus' conquest of the Americas. Deep underground, and unseen for 500 years, are the sacred symbols of a lost culture – they include many bird paintings.

News of Australia's rich avifauna did not begin to reach Europe until the late 18th century, although this continent is home to many of today's most sought-after species: the first budgerigar reached England in 1840, brought back by the great naturalist John Gould, and by the 1850s, imports of budgerigars to England had reached 50,000 birds annually.

Today, bird-keeping is one of the most popular pastimes in the world. After World War II, for example, the British Budgerigar Society had 20,000 members, keeping 4 million budgerigars as household pets. And it is just as popular in many other

Protarchaeopteryx were ground-living therapod dinosaurs that flourished 120 to 150 million years ago. Though flightless, they were clothed in feathers – an interesting link.

The most famous and significant of the ancestral fossils is *Archaeopteryx*, a specimen of which was first discovered in a Bavarian quarry near Solnhofen in 1861. The rocks, formed about 150 million years ago as silt built up in a warm coral lagoon, gradually became compressed into stratified limestone. Within these strata lie exquisitely preserved remains of many of the region's early inhabitants.

About the size and shape of a magpie, *Archaeopteryx* presents a tantalizing blend of avian and reptilian features. Even though modern birds may not have descended from it directly, it nevertheless provides important evidence about avian origins. The Solnhofen skeleton shows clear affinities with reptiles, such as teeth, but also possesses features characteristic of birds: preserved in precise detail, the feathers of Archaeopteryx reveal a structure that is in every way typical of modern birds.

LEFT *A male Violet Budgerigar.*
BELOW Archaeopteryx, *a fossilized blend of reptile and bird.*

parts of Europe and the USA. Some bird shows attract up to 100,000 people to view as many as 14,000 exhibited birds, and 80 per cent of them are canaries. Recent surveys by pet product marketing organizations indicate that at least 40 million canaries are currently kept in Western Europe and the USA alone – it is by far the most popular cage bird in the world.

CONQUERING THE AIR: THE EVOLUTION OF BIRDS

Birds form one of the most conspicuous and familiar groups in the animal kingdom. The features that so clearly set them apart are their adaptations for flight, evolved from an ancient body plan reflecting their descent from reptiles.

Fossil records indicate that birds originated in the Jurassic period when dinosaurs dominated the earth, more than 150 million years ago. Despite the claims of a small but vocal minority, most biologists now agree that modern birds do indeed represent a line of descent that links them directly to the dinosaurs themselves. This view is strongly borne out by recent fossil finds in China. *Caudipteryx* and

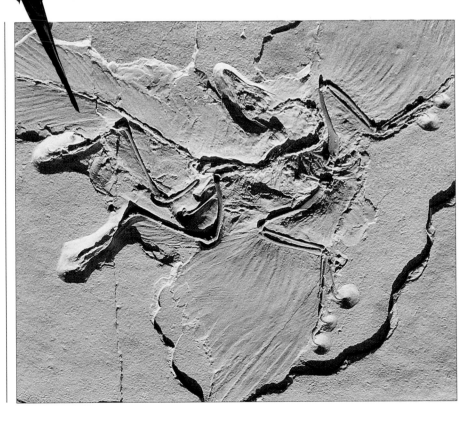

CROSS-SECTION OF A BUDGERIGAR SHOWING CIRCULATION SYSTEMS, BONE AND SOFT TISSUE

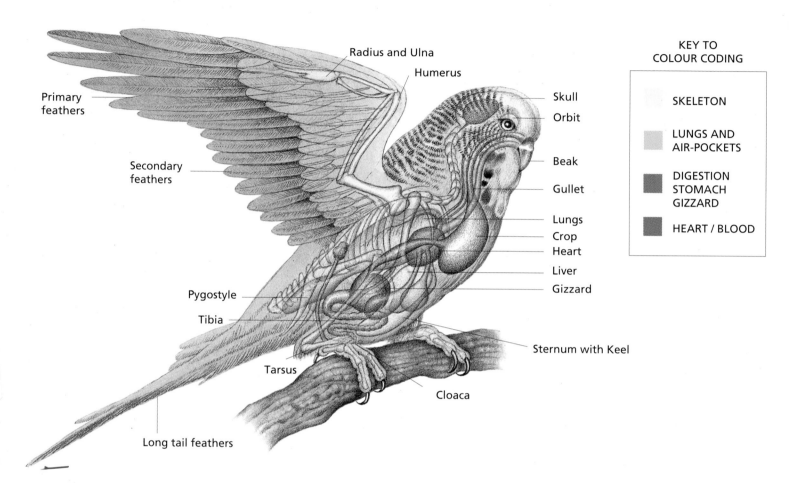

Radius and Ulna
Humerus
Primary feathers
Secondary feathers
Pygostyle
Tibia
Tarsus
Long tail feathers

Skull
Orbit
Beak
Gullet
Lungs
Crop
Heart
Liver
Gizzard
Sternum with Keel
Cloaca

KEY TO COLOUR CODING

SKELETON

LUNGS AND AIR-POCKETS

DIGESTION STOMACH GIZZARD

HEART / BLOOD

The Penguins' feet, although ungainly for walking, provide excellent propulsion for swimming underwater.

CONSTRUCTED FOR FLIGHT

All birds show clear evidence of adaptations evolved for flight. Even birds that today lack this power, such as emus, kiwis and penguins, exhibit evidence that their ancestors once flew.

Over aeons, the skeletons of birds have been refined to provide maximum strength with minimal weight. Unlike our solid bones, those of birds are largely hollow, supported by a critically positioned mechanism of struts and trusses. One of the most striking elements of bird skeletons is the sternum, or breastbone, developed to provide attachment for the muscles that control the wings and power for flight.

The most distinguishing feature of birds is their feathers. These exquisitely detailed structures come in many forms, each adapted to perform a particular role. Formed from keratin and, like other epidermal structures, periodically shed or moulted, feathers are derived from scales similar to those that cover reptiles. Indeed, unmodified scales are found today on the legs of birds. Down feathers (plumules) provide insulation, while contour feathers give the body its aerodynamic shape. Special hair-like feathers form eyebrows, while owls and other nocturnal fliers have whiskers (*vibrissae*) similar to those of mammals.

It is the flight feathers, however, that are the most complex and specialized. The main feather shaft bears rows of barbs on each side, which in turn have rows of tiny barbules that possess rows of hooks (*hamuli*). These hooks link to adjacent barbules and thus the feathers effectively form a smooth, regular surface. As anyone who has examined a flight feather knows, these delicate links can easily be broken and reformed. Preening is the bird's way of servicing and maintaining a smooth surface layer and effectively distributing oily secretions from the uropygial gland at the base of the tail, which render the feathers waterproof.

The original function of feathers was probably insulation to conserve body heat. It is noteworthy that, at around 43°C (109°F), birds maintain a significantly higher temperature than mammals. This may, in turn, reflect a more active metabolism, for flying demands energy.

Without its characteristic covering of feathers, the body of a bird appears clumsy and awkward. Feathers provide the bird with a smooth profile that is aerodynamically efficient without adding much weight. Nowhere is this more apparent than on the wings. The bones of the wings provide little more than attachment points for the flight muscles. The critical aerofoil shape of a wing generates lift and is wholly formed from strong, flexible flight feathers.

An additional function of feathers is that of display and coloration. For some birds this means camouflage and concealment, but in many species it is just the opposite. In the intense competition for mates and reproductive success, an increasingly gaudy plumage has evolved in numerous species, designed for self-promotion and demonstrating fitness. The brightest plumage is generally confined to males – the females and young remain drab to avoid attracting attention, particularly during the breeding season when they are most vulnerable.

PHYSIOLOGY

Adaptations to flight are not confined to structural or mechanical features, however. The way in which a bird's body functions has also been modified over time. Flight, in particular flapping flight, is a high-energy form of movement, so it is not surprising that birds have evolved many ways to improve efficiency and minimize effort. Thus, some birds, such as albatrosses and vultures, have evolved long, narrow wings that allow them to exploit thermals and other air movements, soaring for hours without wasting energy to flap.

More fundamental still are adaptations of the respiratory system, which greatly enhance the efficiency with which oxygen enters the blood stream and carbon dioxide is removed. In our own lungs air ebbs and flows with each breath, some remaining behind with each cycle. Respiration in birds involves a far more efficient one-way circulation of air. The lungs themselves are relatively small and inelastic, but they are supplemented by a series of air sacs, some of which even occupy space within the long bones. By controlling airflow through the sacs, a one-way circulation is achieved that fully flushes the lungs on each breath.

With the higher rate of metabolism needed for powered flight comes a corresponding increase in body temperature. The complex airflow through a bird's body also efficiently removes excess metabolic heat.

The bird's circulatory system, too, has adapted to provide maximum blood flow to the flight muscles. Not only is the heart particularly large and powerful, but it also beats faster than similarly sized mammalian hearts.

*The Cape Vulture (*Gyps coprotheres) *is well adapted to soaring flight.*

*The European Robin (*Erithacus rubecula) *in flight, showing the extremities of wing movement.*

FLIGHT

In the course of evolution, the ability to glide has arisen independently, quite a number of times, among unrelated groups of animals, such as flying lizards, flying squirrels and even an Australian spider. Powered flight, though, may only have arisen on three or four occasions.

The earliest fliers were insects that took to the air during the Carboniferous period, about 400 million years ago. They were followed some 200 million years later by the Pterosaurs, a group of early reptiles. Some of these had wingspans of up to 12m (40ft), which suggests that beyond simple gliding, their flying abilities were limited. Far more recently, bats took to the air, making up for their late start by developing a superior ultrasonic echolocation system that allows them to compete successfully alongside birds and insects.

Birds, bats and insects fly in very different ways, and present separate evolutionary means of becoming airborne. Unlike insect flight, which is unimaginably complex, bird flight is relatively straightforward and can largely be explained in terms of conventional steady-state fluid dynamics.

A Eurasian Bullfinch (Pyrrhula pyrrhula) *about to land, showing an oblique wing angle. The wing-tip feathers are widely spaced to control air flow and prevent stalling.*

Central to bird flight is a phenomenon known as 'Bernoulli's principle', after the 18th-century Swiss mathematician who formulated it. Viewed in cross-section, the top surface of a wing is curved more than the bottom, making the distance from leading edge to trailing edge longer above than beneath. This means that air flowing over the top of the wing must travel faster than the air passing underneath. Bernoulli's principle depends upon the fact that the faster the air is flowing, the lower the pressure it exerts. From this it becomes apparent that a region of low pressure, formed above the wing, provides lift.

Due to the pressure difference between the two wing surfaces, air will naturally curl past the trailing edge and around the wing tips to equalize the pressure. As a result, the smooth flow of air over the wing is interrupted, creating turbulence. This appears as vortices trailing behind the wing, particularly from the wing tips. For maximum lift to be generated, it is necessary to control the airflow and keep it as smooth and regular as possible.

Aeronautical engineers have incorporated similar elements in the wings of modern aircraft to maintain airflow and improve lift. One particularly important component of an aeroplane wing is the leading-edge slot, which opens up at low speeds (during take-off or landing). The greater angle the wing presents to the air at this time causes airflow over the top of the wing to separate, causing a sudden and drastic loss of lift – a condition known as stalling. The slot that opens along the leading edge feeds extra air into the low-pressure region to smooth the flow, preventing turbulence and maintaining lift.

In birds, the alula, or bastard wing, anatomically similar to the human thumb, acts in exactly the same way as an aircraft's leading-edge slot to control airflow over the wing. It is interesting that there are only two groups of non-flightless birds – the loon and the hummingbird – in which the alula is missing.

In the case of loons (*Gavidae*), a rather primitive group of birds that are inexpert, slow fliers, it appears that the need for such aerodynamic refinement has not yet arisen during their evolution. At the other end of the spectrum are the hummingbirds, whose flight has evolved beyond the point where such slots are effective; in terms of aerodynamics, their complex flight mechanism is probably more closely related to that of insects and helicopters.

HOW ARE BIRDS NAMED?

Closely linked with classification is nomenclature, the system of naming plants and animals.

Scientific nomenclature of plants and animals is based upon the method proposed by the Swedish naturalist Carl von Linn (*Carolus Linnaeus*) in 1758. This is a binomial (two-part name) system based on Latin, the international language of science at the time. The first part of the name indicates the genus and the second the species. Thus the Rainbow Lorikeet is known as *Trichoglossus haematodus*, a name that refers to its spiny, nectar-feeding tongue and bright underwing colouring (tricho = hairlike; glossa = tongue; haematodus = blood red).

This species occurs over a wide area, stretching from Tasmania through the islands of the Indonesian archipelago and beyond. To handle this diversity, each form has been given its own subspecific scientific name. Thus *T. haematodus moluccanus* (Swainson's or Blue Mountain Lorikeet) is found in Tasmania and Eastern Australia, while *T.h. haematodus* (Green-naped Lorikeet) is confined to New Guinea and the south Moluccan islands.

This profusion of subspecific names is not unusual; among cage and aviary birds, even within a single taxon (taxonomic group, see box right), a number of distinctive varieties or mutations may be recognized, each with its own name.

There are several reasons why scientific names are necessary. Countries tend to have their own particular names for species occurring within their borders, and even in English, common names can be both variable and misleading. Different names may be used to describe the same species in adjacent areas, while the same name is sometimes applied to a variety of quite different birds.

Robins in Europe, America and Australia, for example, are totally unrelated to each other. This has led to a proliferation of unwieldy and confusing vernacular names – such as Red-fronted Flowerpecker Weaver Finch – which are no easier to remember than their scientific counterparts.

Another difficulty with vernacular names is the absence of uniformity and regulation, which frequently causes confusion to the layperson. The formulation and use of scientific names, in contrast, is strictly monitored and controlled by international agreement to eliminate confusion and ambiguity.

Two lorikeets, each with their own subspecific scientific name: Goldie's Lorikeet (Trichoglossus goldiei), ABOVE, *and Swainson's Lorikeet* (Trichoglossus haematodus moluccanus), LEFT.

HOW ARE BIRDS CLASSIFIED?

Birds exist on all continents, and come in a bewildering array of forms and colours. Biologists try to make order of this diversity by arranging organisms systematically into a hierarchy that unites like with like, and at the same time attempts to reflect evolutionary relationships. As our understanding of birds and their biology improves (for example through DNA analysis), the way in which we arrange and classify them is refined – one of the reasons why books sometimes appear to disagree on names and classification (also known as taxonomy, or systematics).

The major divisions of the bird world – categories such as parrots, grebes, penguins and woodpeckers – are called 'orders', and comprise some 27 distinctive groups. Each order is subdivided into a number of families: thus the lories, cockatoos and parrots, all clearly related to one another in a single order (referred to in aviculture as 'parrotlike'), are nonetheless sufficiently distinct from each other to be recognized as three separate families. Families are subdivided into genera, which, in turn, are made up of one or more species.

A species is the fundamental building block of evolution, and hence classification, but it is often unclear where one species ends and another begins. As a result, extensive minor subdivisions (called subspecies, races, variations, morphs and colour forms) exist besides the more than 8 000 recognized bird species. These categories have no sound biological basis and are often highly subjective; some may eventually become species, while many others do not occur in the wild but exist solely as a result of selective breeding.

LIVING WITH BIRDS

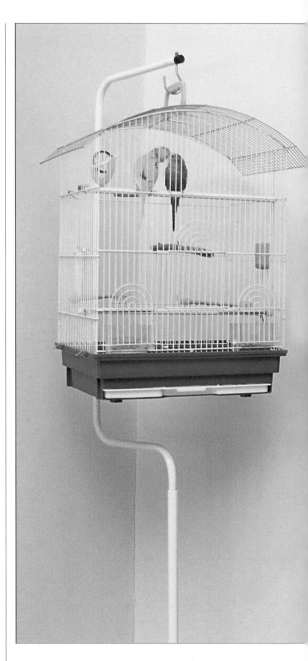

For most people, bird-keeping stems from the simple desire to own a pet and experience the joy of sharing one's home with another living creature and its beautiful plumage or song. For others, especially the elderly, a bird offers companionship; and caring for a bird will teach children about life and responsibility.

But before you buy a bird on impulse, take time to assess what pet-owning involves. Remember that any pet brings a multitude of obligations as well as pleasures. Trapped in an alien environment, a bird is utterly dependent on its owner, who determines and controls its quality of life.

So make sure, for example, that you have the necessary resources and enough time and commitment to care for a bird – not only when it is well. Parrots, in particular, can become extremely attached to one individual and very resentful when left alone. (This is particularly true for hand-reared birds.) Bird-keeping can become an all-consuming passion, and the time spent with your birds could undermine domestic harmony (especially when family duties are neglected). Before you introduce any pet into your family, discuss potential problems and agree upon solutions in advance.

You may also need to discuss potential problems with your neighbours: some birds, particularly parrots and their relations, have loud, raucous voices.

ABOVE *Macaws and cockatoos make a colourful display.*
TOP *Coloured Canaries.*
OPPOSITE BELOW *The Palm Cockatoo* (Probosciger aterrimus) *is a rare species.*
PREVIOUS PAGES *Pet birds, such as this Sulphur-crested Cockatoo, captivate people of all ages.*

There are species that choose to sing vociferously at first light, when most people are trying to sleep, while others, such as many of the parrots, will emit loud and raucous alarm calls at the least disturbance. You and your family may be prepared to accept such disturbance, but your neighbours may not be as tolerant. In many countries there are strict regulations governing noise, and failure to observe the rules may result in severe penalties. Even when you are within the law, pay attention to maintaining harmonious relationships with those who live nearby.

Budgerigars make ideal family pets – they amuse young and old alike, without complicated upkeep.

CHOOSING YOUR BIRD
BIRDS AS PETS

Think carefully about which type of bird will be most suited to your situation. Many people choose a budgerigar or canary, as both are easily available in pet shops and relatively inexpensive to buy, house and feed. They satisfy the needs of those who seek the companionship of a pet without complicated upkeep. Both have attractive plumage, simple dietary needs and survive well alone in cages. In addition, the budgerigar can be a great mimic when taught to imitate simple sounds and short, spoken phrases. Canaries, on the other hand, are known for their beautiful song.

Other small members of the parrot family, such as cockatiels, are also popular pets. They, too, are good mimics and tolerate handling by humans. The larger cockatoos, macaws and parrots are more demanding and not suitable for beginners; they are also significantly more expensive. Those that have been hand-reared invariably

RIGHT *The Greater Hill Mynah* (Gracula religiosa), *if trained early enough, can become quite tame.*
BELOW *An outdoor aviary well suited to an 'island' site, showing a good level of protection against sun and rain.*

make the best pets; in fact, few birds become really tame unless in constant human company or handled by humans from the time that they hatch.

Another popular bird, renowned for its ability to mimic human speech and familiar sounds, is the Greater Hill Mynah. If trained early, it can become tame and acquire an impressive repertoire. It is not fond of being handled, though. Give some consideration to finches, too. These can be brightly coloured and often gregarious. They are best kept in larger accommodation, such as indoor or outdoor aviaries, and prefer the company of other finches.

LEFT *These Roller Singing Canaries are judged on the quality of their song. Prior to judging, the doors on their cages are closed, allowing the birds to roost. When the doors are opened, the birds awake and, thinking it is dawn, begin to sing.*
BELOW LEFT *Peaceful Dove singing competitions are held regularly in Bali. The cages are raised to the top of high bamboo poles to simulate a high song-post – the position chosen by the birds when they claim territory in the wild.*
BELOW *The cages for bird-singing competitions in Bali are highly decorative.*

COMPETITION BIRDS

People who breed birds for show and competitions tend to concentrate on producing specimens that approach the ideal qualities of form and condition set by a show standard. They seldom experience any close attachment to the birds, which are usually kept secured in a locked bird room or aviary; they are rarely treated as pets. Any bird that fails to achieve perfection as a competition or show specimen or prove useful to the breeder is likely to be passed on to other enthusiasts or sold as a pet.

Success in the domain of breeding to type calls for good bird-keeping skills and requires an understanding of the complex world of practical genetics. Although luck can play a role, allowing early triumphs, it can also take years to build up a good stud and achieve the high standards required.

A good place to start is by approaching a successful competitive breeder, or joining one of the specialist clubs. They can advise on where to obtain the best stock and how to achieve the best results. There is no substitute for having good, well-informed friends to whom one can turn for advice.

FOREIGN AND UNUSUAL BIRDS

Although most novice bird-keepers are prudent and start with the more common and simple-to-manage species, there always exists the temptation to be different and acquire unusual birds. Sadly, some people still believe that they gain social status by owning rare or dangerous wildlife. Yet they fail to recognize the responsibilities this brings, and the birds and animals frequently have to suffer the consequences.

Rather start simple, and build gradually upon experience. It is always wise to start with birds that have a long history of domestication before moving to more challenging species.

Raising an uncommon, exotic species is certainly an attractive challenge, though; added to the pleasure of keeping decorative or unusual birds is the satisfaction of knowing that one's efforts can contribute to knowledge about the species and help preserve its wild populations.

RIGHT *Trapping for bird-keeping is a major cause of the decline of the Bali Starling* (Leucopsar rothschildi). BELOW *The White-necked Mynah* (Streptocitta albicollis) *is now very rare. It should be kept only by those intent on breeding it in captivity.*

Before buying exotic or foreign birds, it is important that they be correctly identified and their place of origin determined. In this way each can be paired with a member of its own geographical race – to avoid hybridizing. If you want your birds to breed, try to obtain true pairs. Always choose local, aviary-bred specimens rather than imported ones, because they are usually stronger and healthier and unlikely to be suffering from the stresses of recent importation.

Quarantine and acclimatization procedures must be strictly adhered to so that losses are avoided. Not only can the new acquisition be lost to stress and disease, but birds already in the aviary may suffer the same fate.

To get started you will need a well-designed aviary (see pp44–51) or an environmentally controlled bird room (see pp42–43). Remember that your birds may have been captured in the wild, and would have been subjected to the trauma of trapping and transportation and have been brought to an alien environment with unfamiliar food. All your skill and knowledge will be necessary to acclimatize them to their new home. Sadly, it is at this stage that many such birds die.

INDIGENOUS SPECIES

Indigenous species have been kept in cages and aviaries since bird-keeping began. In many parts of the world, where importation is restricted and other birds are difficult to come by, indigenous birds are still popular. In other countries, however, the possession of indigenous species is now strictly regulated and allowed only under licence to prevent further trapping of wild specimens. Even so, there are many dedicated aviculturists devoted to breeding and exhibiting aviary-bred birds that also live in the wild in their own country. Such birds are often available for sale, but you would be wise to check the local regulations before entering this field.

ABOVE *Australia enforces restrictions on the export of all its indigenous species, even the very common wild budgerigar now bred in millions in captivity throughout the world.*
LEFT *In the UK, the indigenous Goldfinch (Carduelis carduelis) was once trapped in huge numbers. They are now bred by dedicated aviculturists.*

ACCOMMODATION

Just like humans, birds need regular exercise to remain healthy. This means having enough space in which to fly, not just stretch their wings. Again, like humans, birds are prone to obesity and a multitude of related health problems when they are deprived of exercise. Needs do vary from species to species, so bear this in mind when choosing a bird, and try to give it as much space as possible.

The conventional small cages sold at pet stores invariably provide too little room, even for a single budgerigar or canary. The rule is always to use the largest cage your home can accommodate, and anyone with basic DIY skills can design and build an enclosure. In some countries, the minimum cage size permissible for a particular species is laid down by law (small cages are considered cruel). Special attention must be given to such regulations when birds are to be transported, particularly if international air travel is involved.

Once you have chosen an appropriate enclosure or cage, pay attention to its location. Birds need light and air as well as protection from disturbance. This means keeping them away from small children, other household pets and vermin. Many pet birds have been preyed on by domestic cats and dogs when the owners have been absent. Even when they are caged, the stress posed by an apparent threat can prove fatal to some birds. In any case, it is unfair to subject them to anxiety. It is also important to position the cage so that it is located away from draughts and its occupant can find shade from the sun.

It is unnatural for most birds to endure the long waking hours kept by some families. They may be woken at first light by one family member and kept up late into the night by another. Your bird will fare a lot better if you give its day a natural length and darken its cage at night with a blanket or towel.

Besides size and location, the design of the cage must be considered. Most parrots, for example, have powerful beaks and could quickly demolish a wooden cage. The strength and size of the mesh and the spacing of bars must be such that the bird cannot escape or become trapped. Obviously, sharp edges must be avoided and proper provision made for easy cleaning and the removal of droppings. Some birds, such as Greater Hill Mynahs, are messy eaters and defecators, scattering their debris widely. If not cleaned regularly, this can attract vermin and encourage harmful bacteria. In addition, birds shed

LEFT *Wood and bamboo cages are common in the Far East.*
BELOW LEFT *Cages incorporating high-sided bottom trays help contain litter.*
BELOW *Large mobile cages provide more space for the occupants and a convenient method of moving them around.*
OPPOSITE BELOW *Aviaries are essential for many species of birds and give them space and freedom to exercise.*

fragments of skin and feathers. If not controlled, this dust and debris can cause allergies and even serious lung infections in some people. To contain the mess within the cage, choose a bottom tray with high side walls or fit clear plastic side guards. Commercial cages of this design are readily available.

In an attempt to improve the lifestyle of their pets and provide exercise opportunities, some bird-keepers allow their birds to fly through the house unattended. Not only does this greatly increase the risk of escape, but it can also result in extensive damage both to the bird and to furnishings, electrical wiring, and much else. All are liable to be attacked and chewed! As for the bird itself, it will eventually need to be put back into its cage and the process of recapture may prove very stressful.

ETHICS AND THE LAW

The demand for cage and aviary birds has spawned a thriving cottage industry in rural areas of China, Indonesia, Thailand and elsewhere. Enormous numbers of wild birds are caught annually. Most change hands in local markets, where a huge proportion succumbs to the traumas of capture, transportation and inadequate care. Yet, the slaughter continues because of demand. As populations of wild birds decline and the value of captive birds increases, illegal trafficking becomes increasingly profitable for the dealers who control it. The rarer and more endangered a species, the higher its price on the black market and, in some societies, unfortunately, the greater the status conferred by ownership of such a bird. Although many governments have enacted legislation to protect their wildlife, enforcement is difficult, particularly in countries where rural poverty is rife. The temptation of substantial profit has led to a flourishing black market in rare and protected birds, which are regularly smuggled throughout the world despite heavy penalties and mounting vigilance by the enforcement agencies. Traffic in wildlife, including birds, is controlled by international agreement under the Convention on International Trade in Endangered Species (CITES), and loopholes in the law, openly flouted by the unscrupulous, are being closed by improved detection.

This places a growing ethical burden on birdkeepers, who must learn to temper their personal desire for the rare and exotic by refusing to buy any but captive-bred stock.

Within most countries, wild bird species are protected and it is illegal to trap, or hold them in captivity, without the appropriate licence. Fortunately, special licences can be obtained by serious breeders to maintain the genetic diversity of their aviary-bred birds. It is up to the individual breeder to become familiar with the regulations of his or her country. Detailed, up-to-date information on legislation regarding any species of wild birds in captivity should be sought from your local government authority.

The ultimate aim of the serious aviculturist should be to breed from his or her own birds, thereby producing fresh stock that can supply the demand for captive birds without endangering the shrinking and vulnerable wild populations. The challenge of raising new generations gives purpose and direction to birdkeeping, as well as making the hobby more enjoyable and lucrative.

RIGHT *A bird market in Indonesia. Unfortunately, many wild birds, illegally trapped, change hands in similar local markets.*
BELOW *Before strict regulations, it was common to see linnets kept in tiny cages, such as these birds in Malta.*

CHAPTER THREE

OBTAINING YOUR BIRDS

*PREVIOUS PAGES Birds such
as this Blue-and-Yellow Macaw
(Ara ararauna) are frequently
hand-reared by dedicated breeders
and can become remarkably tame.
BELOW Children exploring the
bird section of a pet shop.*

WHERE TO FIND BIRDS

Your local pet shop is always a good place to start –
many stock budgerigars, canaries, lovebirds, cockatiels and the more common domesticated finches.

Bird-keepers and breeders often have surplus
stock that may offer a more varied choice; although
the birds may lack the qualities required for exhibition or breeding, they can make ideal pets. To find
such sources, visit local bird shows and look in the
newspapers. Specialist pet and avicultural publica-
tions are a good source of information, too, and
advertisements on community notice boards can
help you locate bird-keepers, unwanted pets and
bird-keeping accessories.

Bird farms specialize in the breeding and sale of
birds. Some provide a wide variety from many continents, while others tend to focus on areas such as the
import of foreign species only.

WHAT TO LOOK FOR

HEALTH

The state of your bird's health is of primary concern,
and the time taken to examine potential stock is
never wasted. A bird in good health will be alert and
active, responding immediately to the slightest disturbance. A bird that is fluffed up and unresponsive
could indicate a problem, although such behaviour is

*TOP Double-eyed Fig Parrots
(Opopsitta diophthalma).*

not necessarily a sign that something is wrong. Young
birds and those under stress often react in this way,
even when they are generally in good health.

Plumage

Worn, slightly abraded plumage does not necessarily
imply poor health. Wild-caught birds in particular
can often appear in poor condition, especially after
a long journey. Damage of this kind is normally
corrected at the next moult. However, always be on
the look-out for signs of French Moult and other

Owning a bird teaches youngsters about commitment and responsibility – while having fun.

viral feather infections (see p78), which may be fatal, and can quickly sweep through an entire collection of birds with devastating results. Conversely, don't be confused by self-inflicted feather loss, common in unhappy parrots and cockatoos. Although not evidence of an infection, such mutilation does reveal psychological problems, which are extremely difficult to correct.

Weight

Weight loss is not always obvious. It can indicate nothing more serious than an inadequate diet, but it can also be the first sign of a growing tumour or the presence of chronic fungal disease.

Bills and claws

Bills and claws can sometimes reveal whether a bird has been well cared for or not – which, incidentally, says much about the seller or previous owner.

LEFT *A healthy Gouldian Finch* and BELOW, *the same type but with a deformed bill.*

Clear signs of attachment in this pair of Fawn-pied Zebra Finches.

THE QUICK 'CHECK-UP'

Experience always provides the best guide to condition, but these signs may indicate that all is not well.

- The bird should be alert and should respond to mild disturbance – it should not be sitting motionless, hunched and fluffed up in the corner of the cage.
- The bird's breathing should be silent and unaccompanied by movement. Any wheezing or tail-bobbing is evidence of disease or parasites.
- Blocked or unevenly sized nostrils could indicate disease.
- Eyes should be bright, without any evidence of discharge.
- In many species a good indication of age is iris colour. Young birds tend to have darker irises that lighten as the bird matures. A stamped, closed leg band applied soon after hatching is usually the only irrefutable way of telling when a bird was born.
- Distorted, stunted feathers and patches of feather loss, particularly on the wings, may indicate viral feather infections.
- Feather-plucking may indicate psychological distress.
- Weight loss is best detected by feeling the state of the flight muscles. If it is possible to feel the keel of the breastbone on either side, there are grounds for suspicion.
- The presence of stains around the cloaca, together with the state of faecal deposits, provide evidence of digestive problems.
- While examining the bill of budgerigars, look carefully for tell-tale tracks left by the mites that cause scaly-face. Provided the infection has not been left untreated (causing permanent damage to the bill), it can easily be treated. However, as the mites spread rapidly, the affected bird or birds should be confined to strict quarantine.

Cinnamon Grey Green Spangle cock budgerigar.

Parrots that have been deprived of suitable sticks to chew on can develop an overshot upper bill, while birds whose claws have been allowed to grow long and straggly have clearly not received the regular manicuring they need.

BONDED PAIRS

If you intend to breed from the stock you are selecting, watch for signs of attachment that indicate pair-bonding behaviour, such as mutual preening. It is wrong to separate a pair that has already bonded. Today, many suppliers will guarantee a bird's gender (at a price), and this is certainly a wise precaution to take when buying expensive birds. It is now also possible to confirm the sex of a bird chromosomally from a single feather, and any seller of an expensive bird should not object to such a test before purchase.

TRANSPORTING YOUR NEW PET HOME

Once you have chosen your pet, you need to arrange its arrival at its new home and a suitable enclosure for the journey. (You should, in fact, have planned for this some time in advance, making sure that suitable accommodation is ready to receive the eagerly awaited newcomer.)

In the bird markets of Southeast Asia, purchases are regularly taken home in brown paper bags, but something more substantial is usually called for – and laws in many countries lay down specific requirements. Since most birds are disturbed by travelling in the open, an uncovered cage is not suitable; a totally enclosed, darkened box is better. For small birds such a box can be made of cardboard, but larger, more powerful birds such as parrots could soon escape. In general, boxes for transportation should be small to prevent the occupants from moving about and injuring themselves, and each bird should have its own compartment to prevent squabbling.

Most birds won't need to feed during the journey. Small nectar-feeders, however, will require special consideration; they need a food supply and a perch, as well as regular rest periods when they can be exposed to light in order to feed.

LEFT *An airfreight packing case for birds minimizes travel trauma.*

INSET *This carrying carton is suitable only for small birds – larger, more powerful birds could soon escape.*

For many of us, moving house is a stressful event, and birds, too, can find it traumatic; it is important, therefore, to try to keep stress levels to a minimum. Careful handling of travelling boxes or cages is essential, as is keeping the birds as quiet as possible. This is not always possible with store-purchased birds, however; they are better prepared by the addition of probiotics to their diet (see pp82–83).

Preparing birds for international air travel is an altogether more complex undertaking. It is strictly regulated, and there are many rules to be complied with and copious documentation to be completed. Regulations vary from country to country, so it is best left to professional shipping companies.

SETTLING IN

No bird should be added to existing stock without undergoing a period of quarantine or isolation. Even a bird that appears healthy can carry parasites or disease, and the condition may become manifest only as a result of the stress during transportation.

Yet there are many other reasons why new birds should be kept separate for a week or two. Only when your bird is in its own cage can you be sure that it is eating properly, for example. Unfamiliar surroundings and a change in diet can affect a bird's appetite, leading to a loss in condition. In this weakened state, it would be far more susceptible to bullying by established, territorial occupants of an aviary. Bullying can sometimes become a major problem, particularly if there are bonded pairs present. When this happens, the best solution is to remove all birds from the aviary for a few days before putting them back in with the newcomer – the original occupants will have lost their earlier territorial advantage.

When birds are moved over long distances, it is possible that their environmental conditions will change considerably. For many species this may be a normal occurrence (as in annual migration), though not over the short time span of an airline flight.

Tropical birds transported from their natural environment can undergo great changes in temperature, humidity and day length. In such cases, you need to make provision for a period of acclimatization. Initially, unacclimatized birds must be kept in conditions similar to those they were used to, until they have overcome the stresses of moving. Away from the tropics, and depending on the time of year, this may involve several weeks of heated accommodation with controlled lighting, accompanied by a familiar diet and probiotic medication. Once the birds have settled in and appear healthy, they can slowly be accustomed to the natural conditions of their new environment. Even at this stage, their new home may present environmental conditions too severe for them to endure throughout the year. Many small tropical birds, for instance, cannot withstand the harsh winters of countries far away from the equator, in which case sheltered and heated winter accommodation is the only option.

CHAPTER FOUR

HOUSING YOUR BIRDS

PREVIOUS PAGES *Although love-birds often bicker and fight when kept in a colony such as this one, this group is happy and content.*

ABOVE *Domesticated cage birds such as budgerigars may be quite happy in a spacious cage, but they must not be overcrowded.* TOP *A typical wooden cage found in the Far East.*

Keeping birds in captivity imposes a special responsibility upon you, the bird-keeper, if your birds are to remain healthy and content. And at the same time, you will only really be able to appreciate your charges if you allow them to display their natural beauty and abilities to the full.

Above all, your bird must have enough room to stretch its wings – whether it is a pet canary in a cage or a condor in an aviary. (This rule is law in many countries and applies at all times and under all circumstances, except for birds in transit or at exhibitions.) Every day birds should be allowed the freedom to fly at least several wing beats if they are to remain healthy, so they should be housed in the largest aviary possible within the constraints of economy, space and the birds' safety.

Although for centuries domesticated birds have been kept for the beauty of their plumage or song, and have gradually grown accustomed to the secure cage environment, many would not hesitate to fly off into freedom should the opportunity present itself. Even so, countless domestic varieties now breed freely in caged accommodation and seem reluctant to fly when they are introduced to the more spacious quarters of an aviary.

PET BIRDS IN CAGES

There are several possibilities for housing birds within the home. These range from a simple cage for a canary or budgerigar to an entire room devoted to a pair of parrots or even an indoor aviary occupying one side of a living room. The customary open-wire cages cannot be considered suitable homes. However ornate the design, they invariably lack protection from draughts and sunlight and do not allow the bird to hide from perceived threats. If a bird must be caged, box-type cages are the preferred choice.

A large aviary blending in with the environment can be a central feature and a great asset to the larger garden.

Whatever the choice of bird housing, provision must always be made to ensure that the occupant is given an adequate period of darkness to let it sleep each night.

Many bird-keepers provide their pet with the opportunity to exercise by allowing it the freedom to fly around indoors. It is wise, though, to restrict this liberty to a room in which it is familiar. In this way, the bird will get to know the safe perches and the location of its cage, which will make it much easier and less stressful for the bird when you want to confine it again. Make sure that doors, windows and any other escape routes are closed when birds are given their freedom in the home. Similarly, other pets, particularly cats, must be shut out of the room for the duration.

BOX CAGES

A box cage is simply a box structure closed on all sides apart from the wire mesh or barred front. Each cage should have a tray on the base, which is easily withdrawn for cleaning while the birds are still in

COMPONENTS FOR MAKING A BOX CAGE

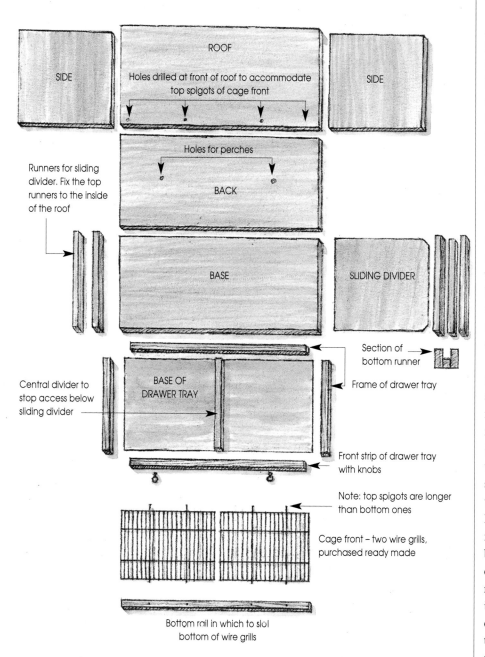

SIDE

ROOF

Holes drilled at front of roof to accommodate top spigots of cage front

SIDE

Runners for sliding divider. Fix the top runners to the inside of the roof

Holes for perches

BACK

BASE

SLIDING DIVIDER

Central divider to stop access below sliding divider

BASE OF DRAWER TRAY

Section of bottom runner

Frame of drawer tray

Front strip of drawer tray with knobs

Note: top spigots are longer than bottom ones

Cage front – two wire grills, purchased ready made

Bottom rail in which to slot bottom of wire grills

residence. For convenience, cages can be provided with removable partitions that can be withdrawn from the front. These allow the cage to be divided for separation of the birds when necessary.

Making a wooden box cage

If you plan to make your own cage from scratch, try to at least purchase a ready-made cage front – this is by far the easiest option. Cage fronts are commercially available in several different sizes, configurations and materials, allowing for easy access and the placing of commercially produced feeders and nest boxes on the front as desired. They are made from stainless steel, plated steel or plastic and have the advantage of being sturdy, burr-free and unlikely to corrode.

Commercially manufactured drinkers and feed containers as well as special clips for cuttlefish bone are all designed for easy fitting to the apertures provided in standard cage fronts. The fitting of the wire bar-type cage front is usually by means of extensions, top and bottom, to some of the cage bars, and these slot into holes drilled into the top and bottom sides of the cage assembly.

If you are building the cage yourself, ensure that adequate space is given for the cage front extensions to fit and drop into the holes provided. The measurement from the outside of the bottom metal rail to the top of the cage bar should be 1.5mm (1/16in) less than the inside measurement from top to bottom of the cage-front aperture in the box structure. The material for the basic box construction is very much dependent on the species to be housed. Any birds that have the habit of chewing into timber, which includes parrotlike species, are better kept in metal cages. Most bird-keepers who choose this type of bird invariably purchase ready-made cages to avoid the more difficult task of working with metal. Fortunately, most of the small domesticated birds and small finches are well suited to a wooden structure, which gives the DIY enthusiast the chance to get busy.

A basic box construction usually comprises waterproof plywood at least 8mm (5/16in) thick, painted with a nontoxic paint after assembly. There are similar materials available that have plastic coatings, such as melamine, and are often more durable and withstand regular cleaning.

OVERVIEW OF THE CONSTRUCTION OF A WOODEN BOX CAGE

1. Make the basic box, allowing the correct space for the cage front (see p40).

2. Fix base to sides with screws and/or wood glue.

3. Drill holes into the bottom rail (lining up the holes with the spigots extending from the cage fronts).

At the back of the cage, drill two holes for the perches – the holes should be slightly larger than the diameter of the perches.

Between the sides, fit the bottom rail. Between this and the back fit the bottom assembled runner. The top runners are fitted onto the inside of the roof.

Twist the perches into the holes at the back of the cage. The perches need regular cleaning, so need to be easily removable.

Assemble the drawer as shown with wood glue and small screws, and ensure that it slides in and out of the cage easily. Similarly, cut and fit the sliding divider.

The perches should fit into the holes provided at the back and slot into the bars of the cage front.

4. Fix the cage fronts by inserting the top spigots upwards into holes drilled in to the cage roof. The cage front can then be pushed down until the spigots line up with the holes in the bottom rail.

5. Remove the cage fronts, drawer and divider. Sand them, then paint with a nontoxic paint. Allow to dry for a couple of weeks to ensure all solvents have evaporated and the paint has hardened. Fit the drawer, slide and any accessories. The cage is now ready for your birds.

Furnishing the box cage
Perches

All cages require some sort of perch, unless the birds are ground birds such as quail (and then a box cage is not really a suitable enclosure). Two perches are essential to allow the bird to flit from one to the other. Although standard, round wooden dowelling for perches is available from pet stores, the regular size does not allow variable perching positions for the feet. Unless a variety of perches is given, the bird may develop foot problems; it is far better to cut natural wood perches from a fruit tree with non-toxic bark – apple or something similar is best. This allows different perch sizes while providing a natural substance to peck at or chew. For many species, branches bearing buds can also provide hours of 'entertainment' and beneficial nourishment. In cases where only proprietary perches are available, use two of different sizes or shapes to ensure some exercise for the feet.

RIGHT Perches can be bought in many thicknesses, which will ensure some exercise for the birds' feet. FAR RIGHT Some types of water and seed feeders – note that a new, unweathered zinc container (BELOW RIGHT) could be toxic. BELOW A typical toy for canaries or budgerigars.

Toys

Birds can suffer from boredom particularly when kept alone, and unless they are occupied in some way, their health can deteriorate. There are many commercially produced 'toys' such as bells, swings and mirrors that can be used, but left in the same place they soon become part of the normal environment and have little purpose.

It is better to occupy the birds by giving them something to peck and chew on, such as twigs with buds or a regular change of natural wood perch. Seed-eaters are well catered for with special seed-chews at which they can nibble and, of course, there are millet sprays that encourage natural foraging. Daily supplies of fresh green food suspended within the cage also serve the same purpose.

Feeding containers

Box cages rarely need more than a standard tubular hopper feeder and a water container placed conveniently near the end of the perch. They should be easily removed for refilling and cleaning.

BIRD ROOMS

A bird room is a room set aside to house several birds each within its own box cage. It can be a free room within your own house or a purpose-built shed in the garden. Bird rooms are essential if you are considering breeding domesticated cage birds either for show or as a stud. In a bird room the birds are secured in a controlled environment and free from disturbances, allowing them to get on with raising their young. A convenient arrangement is a well-ventilated and well-lit outbuilding with one wall taken up by box-type cages. The box cages should have removable dividers to facilitate cleaning and moving birds around.

It is not difficult to construct a multi-tiered arrangement of this type of cage, as many of the components, particularly cage-fronts, are commercially produced. The popularity of bird rooms has spawned the commercial manufacture of numerous designs of cage-front in wood, plastic or metal and in several different sizes and configurations.

The construction of a bird room should receive careful consideration, especially the need to make it vermin- and damp-proof. However careful you may be, bird seed and other foodstuffs act like a magnet to rodents and ants. The floor and plinth walls, therefore, should be made of concrete and should incorporate a waterproof membrane to prevent dampness and rodents from entering from below.

Artificial lighting allows for extended feeding times where winter nights are long. This can be controlled by an electronic timer to dim and switch off automatically at set times. In places where very cold conditions are prevalent the room must be heated, especially when the birds are roosting at night. Thermostatically controlled tubular electrical heaters are ideal for this purpose.

Ventilation becomes increasingly important as the number of birds confined in one room increases: ventilation acts to remove the dust from feathers and seed and to control the humidity. With softbill birds in particular, fungi and moulds can be a problem. Thermally expanding gas struts, as used for controlling the ventilation in greenhouses, are a cheap and effective method of opening and closing windows or vents; a mesh-protected extractor fan can also be used. Additional dust control can be achieved through the use of ionizers – they extract pollen and airborne infectious micro-organisms as well as benefit bird-keepers who are allergic to dust or suffer from chest infections.

BELOW *The bird room can be a room within your house or a purpose-built garden shed.*

INDOOR AVIARIES

An indoor aviary (LEFT) is an enclosure within a building or even your home in which a group of birds can be housed together. This is frequently the method chosen when the bird-keeper wishes to allow more space for the birds to exercise and show off their colours in flight. It can also provide suitable conditions for the more delicate of tropical species to be kept in colder climates. Hummingbirds and many of the nectar feeders are typical species that are housed in indoor aviaries.

Indoor aviaries offer a secure environment in which conditions can be monitored closely and there is a lower risk of contamination from the infections transmitted by wild birds. This type of aviary is particularly useful for valuable birds that may be at risk from theft or disturbance, and it is also a convenient way of housing birds in a city setting. Once again, though, fresh air, sufficient light and high standards of cleanliness and hygiene are absolutely essential.

Indoor aviaries frequently occupy a spare room or even part of a living-room, but there is no reason why external buildings or conservatories cannot be used. Ventilation can become a problem at times of high temperature, but an extractor fan usually solves this problem. (Make sure it is adequately protected to prevent your birds from flying into or through the fan-blades!)

In glass conservatories, pay particular attention to the provision of shade. Large-leafed pot plants are often sufficient, but it is best to shade a part of the roof. Ideally, the floor should be covered with some impervious membrane such as a vinyl – try to buy the floor covering in one piece, to prevent bacteria and dirt from penetrating between overlapping joins. In this way, cleaning becomes much simpler and causes less disturbance to the birds.

Do not be misled into thinking that noisy birds cannot be heard when they are housed indoors. While sounds may be dampened, loud, raucous calls often penetrate and are transmitted with great clarity through the walls – to the possible annoyance of your neighbours.

Some homes have special conservatories constructed alongside a glazed living-room wall to allow intimate observation of a group of colourful exotic birds. This type of arrangement can provide enormous enjoyment for bird-keepers who wish to live in close proximity to their birds while maintaining a house free from dust, feathers and the food debris that, inevitably, abounds.

OUTDOOR AVIARIES

The outdoor aviary (RIGHT) is by far the most popular form of enclosure, particularly in warmer climes. Similarly, many cage birds are released into aviaries after the breeding season to allow them more exercise and freedom during their annual moult.

But before you embark on the ambitious building project to make an aviary, bear these points in mind:

- Establish whether your local planning regulations permit the type of structure you envisage. It will be distressing to you and your birds if the aviary has to be dismantled.
- Discuss your intentions with your neighbours and find out whether there are any objections.
- The accommodation must be well-suited to the species and changed according to its needs (such as heating requirements, chew-proof fittings, etc).
- The size of the aviary should be sufficient to allow the birds to fly about freely.

Other details of significance:
- Perches should be arranged in such a way that droppings from above cannot fall on birds that are perched lower down.
- Feeding areas must be protected from droppings.
- Windows will create a light and airy atmosphere, but must be covered by wire-mesh panels to deter birds from flying into them and harming themselves. If the windows are broken, the birds may even fly through them.
- Consider installing a controllable sliding hatch positioned at about two-thirds the height of the aviary to allow your birds easy access. A small landing platform on either side of the hatch will make access even easier.
- An external door is necessary for the requisite feeding and cleaning routines. A door between shelter and aviary could prove very useful as a secondary safety entrance. (See Safety entrance on p46.)
- As with bird rooms, artificial lighting and control is a great advantage in aviary shelters that are used for winter accommodation.

Positioning

Outdoor aviaries should ideally be positioned where they can be viewed from the house but not from the road – this will help prevent vandalism and theft. They should also be positioned to avoid extraneous street lighting and illumination from cars passing by at night.

Shelter from wind and driving rain is important, as is the provision of shade. Avoid overhanging trees – falling branches can damage the aviary and droppings from wild birds perched above it will cause contamination. Also build far from any poisonous plants in the vicinity – the leaves, bark or wind-blown and falling seeds may be a danger.

The shelter

In temperate regions, try to provide sheltered accommodation adjacent to the aviary so that more fragile species can be shut in for protection, especially through long winter nights. For acclimatized tropical species, a minimum temperature of around 8–12°C (46–53°F) should be maintained.

Safety entrance

To prevent birds from escaping when the aviary door is opened, incorporate a trapped safety enclosure with its own entrance. A second door, usually positioned opposite the shelter (see above), permits entry into the safety enclosure. Once the outside safety door is closed, entry can be made through the main aviary door without fear of the birds escaping.

This feature can also be incorporated within the shelter to avoid driving the birds out into the external aviary in bad weather. If birds are allowed free access to both shelter and aviary in bad weather and you need access to the shelter, they must be driven into the aviary first and trapped there to prevent escape as you enter the shelter.

Basic construction

Birds cannot distinguish between professional workmanship and a roughshod do-it-yourself job, but in the long-term interests of both bird-keeper and birds, the aviary needs to be a solid construction that will serve for many years. Be sure to use the best quality materials you can afford, as replacement of aviary panels, for instance, can be a thankless task and present a serious disturbance to the birds.

If you have any doubts about your architectural and construction abilities, rather buy the ready-made item. This way you can begin bird-keeping immediately and avoid the never-ending maintenance and loss of your birds through some unforeseen problem.

The base

Whichever type of aviary you choose – indoor or outdoor – a solid base is always advised. It provides stable support for the structure and guards against vermin, and is essential for species such as Burrowing Owls or Motmots that will excavate hollows in the aviary floor.

A concrete base and raised plinth walls with adequate provision for drainage will ensure that rodents cannot gain access from below. This base can be covered with gravel or sand. In the case of large aviaries, where overall concreting is impractical, a plinth wall at a depth of around 60cm (24in) below the surface, covered with a foundation or concrete slab extending 60cm (24in) horizontally outside the aviary, will deter most burrowing mammals.

The roof

Depending on the size of the aviary, the roof structure must adequately support the heaviest load likely to be encountered. The likelihood of heavy snowfalls needs to be considered, as they can overload weak structures. Although wire-mesh should cover the entire aviary roof, it is necessary to cover part of this with translucent sheeting to protect the bathing and feeding areas from the droppings of wild birds and the nesting sites from heavy rain. Sheeting must always be adequately sloped to drain away any rainwater.

Framework and wire-mesh

The construction materials you use for your aviary must be selected according to the birds that are to be housed in it. Certain parrots and parrot-like birds can be extremely destructive and will demolish wooden frames and even wire-mesh covering if it is not strong enough.

Be warned: steel wire-mesh comes in various different grades, the cheaper (and inferior) quality is usually masked by galvanizing. Plastic-coated and stainless-steel varieties, while readily available, are usually more costly.

The gauge of the wire and size of the mesh both need careful consideration, because they have to keep the birds in and pests out. Mice and snakes are able to squeeze through mesh no larger than 12mm (half an inch) square, as can the newly hatched young of small quail species.

MATERIALS FOR CONSTRUCTING A WOODEN OUTDOOR AVIARY

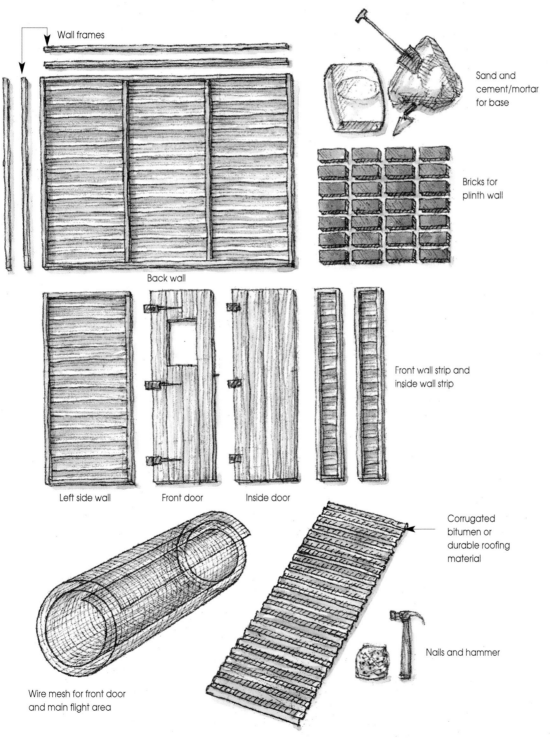

Wall frames

Back wall

Sand and cement/mortar for base

Bricks for plinth wall

Left side wall

Front door

Inside door

Front wall strip and inside wall strip

Corrugated bitumen or durable roofing material

Nails and hammer

Wire mesh for front door and main flight area

OVERVIEW OF THE CONSTRUCTION OF AN OUTDOOR AVIARY

1. Make a plinth of bricks or concrete blocks between 10cm (4in) and 20cm (8in) above ground level. When the mortar has set, cover the floor in between with concrete paving slabs or concrete.

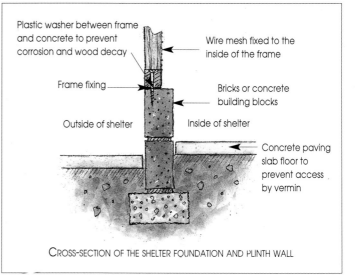

Plastic washer between frame and concrete to prevent corrosion and wood decay

Wire mesh fixed to the inside of the frame

Frame fixing

Bricks or concrete building blocks

Outside of shelter

Inside of shelter

Concrete paving slab floor to prevent access by vermin

CROSS-SECTION OF THE SHELTER FOUNDATION AND PLINTH WALL

2. Construct a wall frame, using metal brackets and screws to secure the corners. Fix overlapping weatherboard or cladding to the frame with nails, ensuring that there are no gaps for rodents to enter or from which birds can escape.

3. Position and fix the wire mesh to the inside surface of the front frames. Then attach the front frames to the rear wall frame with coach screws or nuts and bolts.

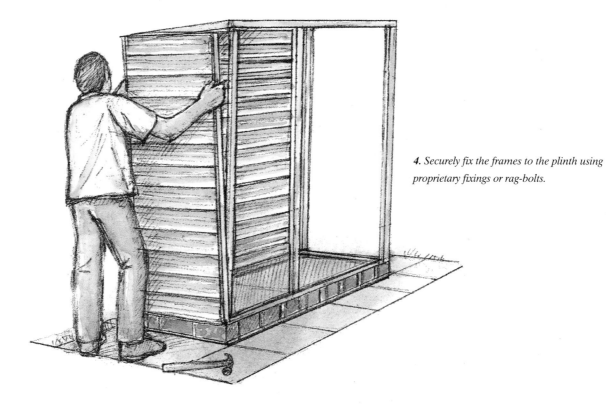

4. Securely fix the frames to the plinth using proprietary fixings or rag-bolts.

5. Fix the roofing material and doors into place. The construction should be sealed with a nontoxic preservative and allowed to dry thoroughly. Finally, manoeuvre a substantial branch into the aviary and secure it with wire before introducing the birds.

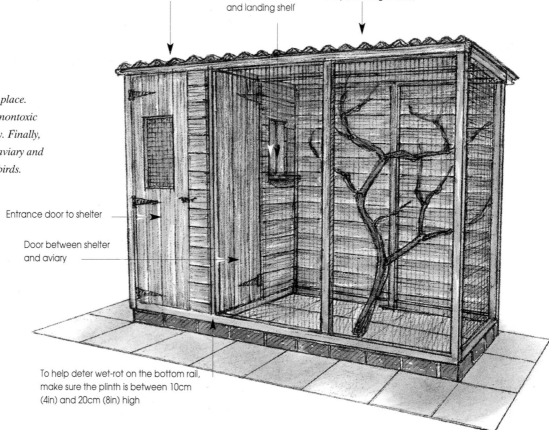

Shelter

Sliding door/hatch and landing shelf

Aviary (main flight area)

Entrance door to shelter

Door between shelter and aviary

To help deter wet-rot on the bottom rail, make sure the plinth is between 10cm (4in) and 20cm (8in) high

RIGHT *The mixed collection of birds in this aviary includes Diamond Doves (Geopelia cuneata), budgerigars, White-backed Mousebirds (Colius colius) and Emerald Doves (Chalcophaps indica).*
BELOW LEFT *A small pond or water container is essential for the birds to clean their plumage.*
BELOW RIGHT *A Cape Turtle Dove (Streptopelia capicola) feeding from a raised platform.*

Water and electrical services

Wherever water and electrical services are incorporated, safety precautions are essential and regulations should be strictly adhered to. Although you may be tempted to cut corners on the installation of these services, there are real dangers associated with external electrical wiring and plumbing.

All electrical wire should be adequately protected, not only from the weather but also from rodents, not to mention the birds themselves. Where parrots are concerned, all accessible wiring should be encased in steel conduits. Hard, plastic conduits may withstand gnawing by rodents but it will not stand up to a parrot's bill. Similarly, plastic water piping is no match for parrot species.

You will frequently wash out your aviary, and fill the baths and water containers using a hosepipe. To ensure that foul water is not accidentally siphoned back into the drinking water main, local authorities may insist that a double-check valve be fitted.

The aviary environment

The function of an aviary is to allow the birds enough space to fly, so filling it with plants to make it look more attractive is defeatist. It is far better to enhance the outside appearance by planting suitable shrubs. There are many attractive and nonpoisonous climbers – such as loniceras and clematis – that will grow fast to cover the wire-mesh, encourage insect life and provide a beautiful show of colourful flowers. Within the enclosure, large pot-grown shrubs should be used to afford hiding places and possible nesting sites.

Aviary plants, perches and nest boxes must suit the species that are going to live among them. Parrots, particularly, are likely to be destructive, and so vegetation is best avoided; perches and nest boxes must be very robust indeed if they are to last any time at all. Toys, too, are chewed to fragments and require regular replacement to keep these birds occupied.

Most other birds are far less destructive, allowing for a more attractive environment and a greater choice of plants to encourage natural activities such as foraging, as well as offering protection and well-hidden nesting sites.

To prevent parasitic worm infestations from the droppings of wild birds, choose an aviary with a bare concrete floor – this can then be washed down

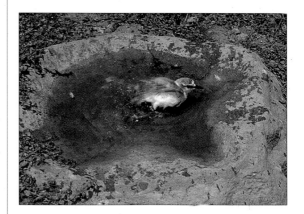

regularly or, perhaps, covered with gravel. If small seed-eaters are being housed, coarse sand can be used, as long as it is washed and dried regularly.

A small pond can be incorporated, but should be positioned under a sheltered roof and cleaned out each day to prevent infections from wild-bird droppings. Choose hopper-type drinking-water containers rather than open bowls, so they cannot be used by the birds for bathing.

in a habit of overturning feeding utensils, they should be fixed, and strong enough to withstand chewing or attack by the more destructive species.

Perches

Apart from their obvious use as seating, perches may provide a platform for copulation, are regularly used in territorial displays and as song posts, and some birds may even benefit from chewing on them. Changes in perch size exercise the birds' feet.

The positioning of perches should be carefully thought out, for it can have a significant effect on the birds' feeding ability and nesting behaviour. Toucans, for instance, need adequate space above the perch to allow them to toss their food into the air before catching it in their open bill; other species may rely on perches for access to their nests.

As a guide, perches of different thickness should be positioned horizontally across the flight line of the aviary, but at a reasonable distance from the boundary to prevent any part of the bird colliding with the wire-mesh or shrubs. For small finches, twigs from different trees – some firm, others flexible – can be suspended throughout the aviary.

Pest deterrents

Unfortunately, outdoor aviaries tend to attract vermin as well as neighbourhood cats. A cat on an aviary roof or even walking close by will often cause panic, particularly among breeding birds, while rodents carry diseases that are transmissible to birds and should be discouraged, particularly near small seed-eaters.

Today, there are many different humane and live traps available that allow you to release your catch again – some distance away. Toxic substances are not advocated, particularly if there is a chance that your birds may consume the poisoned rodent. Rats can be a more serious problem and professional advice should be sought to eliminate them.

The latest development in rodent repellents involves a device that emits high-energy pulses of ultrasonic sound. This deters any pest coming within its range and is most effective – it also works for felines. A different cat deterrent is a PIR (Passive InfraRed) operated spray valve attached to a garden hosepipe. When a cat comes into range it receives a high-pressure jet of water to frighten it away.

Ultrasonic pest deterrents are remarkably effective, emitting bursts of high-energy ultrasonic sound that is inaudible to the human ear but causes disturbance to other mammals such as rodents and cats. Some even deter insects.

Feeding stations

Feeding stations should be positioned either well off the ground (where they cannot be fouled from above) or, in the case of ground birds such as quail, on the ground but protected from other birds' droppings. Ideally, the main feeding station should be within the shelter, but supplementary bowls of food can be placed in different positions in the aviary each day to encourage foraging. Where birds are in

CAGES FOR SPECIAL PURPOSES
Nest boxes, shelves and nesting materials

Some species, such as some parrotlike birds, tits and starlings, use nest boxes (see p132 in chapter eight for more details about nest boxes) throughout the year for roosting purposes, so the nest boxes should be left within the aviary or shelter. For other species that will attempt to nest in aviary conditions throughout the year, the nest boxes must be removed after a second or third fledging to prevent breeding exhaustion.

Competition cages are standardised to ensure fairness. The judge is therefore prevented from presuming an outstanding cage is home to an outstanding bird.

In the more temperate regions, breeding success is far from certain during cold weather and the chances of egg-binding (see pp 80) are increased significantly. Only when the weather warms up should nest boxes and nesting materials be introduced to the aviary.

Show cages

The design of show cages varies considerably, depending on the type or species of bird it is to house and the country in which the show is held. However, within each country and bird show, cage designs are

standardized to ensure fairness of competition. This ensures that the judges cannot identify the bird owner with recognizable or marked cages and that the cage decoration is not taken into consideration.

Show cages are smaller than the birds' normal living accommodation to allow the judges to inspect the birds more closely. Show birds are specially trained to be steady and alert and to maintain their posture at a required standard. Birds should not be kept in these cramped cages any longer than is necessary; this always causes grave concern when shows extend over more than a few days.

A BASIC HOSPITAL CAGE

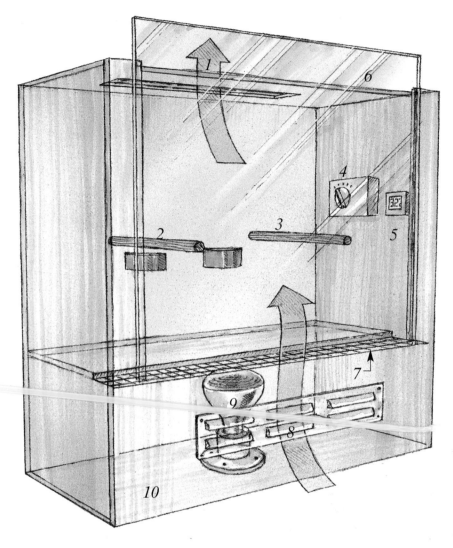

1. Air vent

2. Food and water containers close to perches

3. Perches positioned to give good head and tail clearance, as well as to allow for exercise while flying from one perch to the other

4. Thermostat to control underfloor heating

5. Digital thermometer

6. Sliding glass or clear plastic panel to allow access and good visibility

7. Wire-mesh floor section to allow ventilation and warm air to flow into cage

8. Air vent

9. Infra-red lamp (maximum 60W)

10. The floor should be easily cleanable – stainless steel is ideal, but if wood is used, ensure at least 12.5cm (4.5in) clearance space from the lamp

FEEDING YOUR BIRDS

ABOVE *A nutritious seed block.* TOP A *Eurasian Jay with an acorn, ready to hide it away for winter.*

In the wild, birds have access to a wide choice of food, so if captive birds are to remain healthy and breed successfully, they need to have a similarly diverse and balanced diet.

Birds are traditionally categorized as seed-eaters, fruit-eaters, nectar-feeders, insectivores, and so forth. Do remember, though, that these artificial divisions serve only as a general guide – most birds consume a broad spectrum of foods.

The diet of wild birds is very difficult to assess with accuracy, as it changes seasonally, as different foods become available. Plants come into flower and set seed, and a great number of insects and spiders mature and lay eggs; these foods provide protein, carbohydrates, fats (the main nutritional building blocks), vitamins and minerals.

A bird's nutritional needs change throughout its life. The requirements of young, growing birds are quite different from those of adults and from birds during breeding and egg-laying seasons. Many species also eat more at certain times of the year to store the fat essential for migration, a very energy-demanding activity.

Successful bird-keepers devote considerable effort and ingenuity to ensure that their charges receive an adequate diet. Ill health and poor reproductive success can usually be traced to a dull, repetitive and inadequate diet. In the wild, birds are able to tailor their diet according to availability and need, but this is difficult to mirror in captivity.

Although bird-keepers are advised to offer their birds a variety of natural foods, they may not always be able to do so and must resort to proprietary food additives instead. Since the vitamin and mineral content of store-purchased products is generally unknown, it is wise to buy from a reputable source whose regular turnover guarantees fresh supplies.

Fruit-eating species need a variety of fruit supplied fresh each day.

A BALANCED DIET

CARBOHYDRATES AND FAT

During the digestive process, carbohydrates are broken down into glucose, the primary fuel in the body's metabolic cycle. Surplus carbohydrates are converted into fat, which provides an essential store of energy but can, if laid down in excess, prove damaging to health.

The fat consumed in food contributes important dietary components that are not obtainable elsewhere but nevertheless essential to good health.

PROTEIN

Proteins, classed as complex molecules, are made up of around 20 amino acids; some of these are not manufactured in the body and must be absorbed from food. As animal proteins generally contain larger quantities and a greater diversity of amino acids than plant proteins, even seed-eating birds will become omnivorous periodically, especially during the breeding season. Young birds, in particular, need higher levels of protein for growth. Egg-food is a useful supplement during breeding.

A high-protein crumb supplement.

ESSENTIAL MINERALS

MINERAL	FUNCTION
Calcium	Essential for nerve and muscle function, and for health of hens during breeding and while chicks are growing.
Cobalt	Assists the production of red blood cells.
Copper	Assists haemoglobin production, as well as the development of bones, feathers, skin, nerves and enzymes.
Iodine	Essential for thyroid function and maintaining good condition of arteries.
Iron	Essential for carrying oxygen in the blood.
Magnesium	Assists nerve and muscle function, bone growth and temperature control.
Manganese	Affects sex hormones and fertility, blood and bone formation, nerve function and the use of vitamins and enzymes.
Selenium	Works in conjunction with vitamin E to promote growth and fertility and to control any cancerous development.
Sulphur	Affects fertility, feather quality, and the absorption of protein.
Zinc	Essential in the growth of skin, beak and claws and the formation of feathers. Assists wound healing, enzyme and vitamin activity, digestion and the formation of viable reproductive organs in young birds.

VITAMINS

Besides the major food categories (protein and carbohydrates), living creatures require small quantities of other essential substances. Foremost among these are vitamins and minerals, which are often present in insufficient quantities in the natural foods fed to cage and aviary birds. They must, therefore, be enhanced with supplements specially formulated to correct these deficiencies. Do not exceed the recommended dosages, though, as some vitamins can be harmful if taken in excess.

MINERALS

A well-balanced diet will ensure that birds receive the essential minerals. When deficiencies do occur or when additional minerals become necessary (during moulting or in the breeding season), numerous commercial additives and supplements are available. Adhere to the manufacturer's instructions as overdosing may be extremely harmful.

*A Song Thrush (*Turdus philomelos*) feeding from a branch of elderberries hung up in the aviary.*

THE FUNCTIONS AND SOURCES OF ESSENTIAL VITAMINS

VITAMIN	FUNCTION	AILMENTS CAUSED BY DEFICIENCY	SOURCE
Vitamin A	Assists in the formation and protection of membranes within the body.	Infections, especially of the gut, eyes respiratory and reproductive system (deficiency slow to become apparent as vitamin A is stored in the liver).	Vegetable matter and as a proprietary supplement; seeds are low in vitamin A, so seed-eaters need supplements. Cod-liver oil, wheatgerm, milk, carrots, corn.
B vitamins (B1 – thiamine; B2 – riboflavin; B6 – pyridoxine; B12 – choline; folic acid; niacin, panatothenic acid	Good for metabolism and fundamental for growth and plumage development; nerve function; helps prevent anaemia.	Lethargy, poor appetite, fits; deficiency of vitamin B1 is a cause of nervous disorders.	Sprouting seeds and yeast-based supplements are useful, although folic acid, vitamin B12 and intestinal bacteria all contribute to the synthesis of group B vitamins. It follows that excessive use of antibiotics can be harmful to synthesis. Cod-liver oil, milk, green food.
Vitamin C	Ensures healthy skin and protects against infections.	A form of scurvy; skin infections.	Although most species' requirements for vitamin C are synthesized within the body, certain fruit-eating species need supplements. Most food supplements contain adequate supplies of this vitamin. Various vegetables and citrus fruit.
Vitamin D3	Vital in the absorption of calcium within the body.	Soft bone structure, weak nerves and muscles, egg formation problems.	A naturally synthesized vitamin obtained from the action of ultraviolet light on the feathers. This is obtained from sunlight or specific types of spectrally controlled artificial lighting. Cod-liver oil, milk.
Vitamin E	Functions as an anti-oxidant, prevents blood toxicity and helps metabolism and growth. Thought to promote fertility.	Kidney disease, wasting and low fertility,	Wheatgerm oil and food supplements.
Vitamin K	Beneficial for energy storage and blood clotting; helps prevent overeating and haemorrhaging; speeds up wound healing.	Overeating, poor wound healing and haemorrhaging.	In most species vitamin K is synthesized by intestinal bacteria. However, certain species, such as parakeets and fig parrots, suffer from deficiencies. It can be obtained as a food supplement. Green food, roots, liver; soya beans.

BIRD FOODS

The foods described below are widely used by bird-keepers. The list is far from exhaustive, though, and many alternatives may be available in your area (this is particularly true for the tropics, where various fruits and insects are abundant and cheap but cannot be obtained in colder climates).

SEEDS

The variety of seeds available to bird-keepers is enormous, but for many the practical choices are limited by the stocks of the local seed merchants. Although the premixed seed assortments sold in pet shops offer diversity, this may prove a wasteful way to buy. Many bird-keepers prefer to buy from specialist bird-seed merchants to enable them to provide a variety of seeds in separate containers; birds can then feed on the seeds of their choice.

It is important to ensure that the seeds you offer provide a balanced diet, and are clean and in good condition. When given a free choice, some birds will consume excessive amounts of one kind only. For this reason feeding habits should always be monitored.

Millet and canary-grass seed

Cereal crops provide a major source of seeds, with millet being particularly important. Recognizable by their small, spherical seeds, a mixture of millet species from different regions can provide a broad spectrum of nutrients. Other cereals of value include varieties of rice, oats and canary-grass seed (*Phalaris canariensis*). The latter is a grass seed and quite distinct from canary seed (*Canarium spp.*), a large nut of the same name often used as parrot food in Australia and Southeast Asia.

Maize

Another important cereal is maize (corn), which provides a valuable source of vitamin A. In its dry form, maize can be eaten only by the larger parrots, so it is customary to soak or boil it first. Once softened, it can be fed to a variety of birds. Coarsely ground (kibbled) maize is often available from seed merchants and can be fed to chickens, pheasants and pigeons. Corn-on-the-cob is relished by many birds.

Sunflower seed

Sunflowers are widely cultivated for their oil. This, together with their high protein content, makes these seeds an important source of bird food. The white seeds have a higher protein content and less fat than the black or striped seeds, but are significantly more costly.

Hemp seed

Hemp (*Cannabis sativa*) seeds are a popular and smaller alternative to sunflower seeds because of their high-energy properties.

Pine nuts and safflower, rape, maw and teasel seed

Other seeds with a high fat content include safflower seeds, a number of rape seed varieties and pine nuts. Blue maw (poppy), teasel and other, less familiar, species are sometimes recommended as supplementary diets for some species.

Large seed hoppers made from plastic buckets.

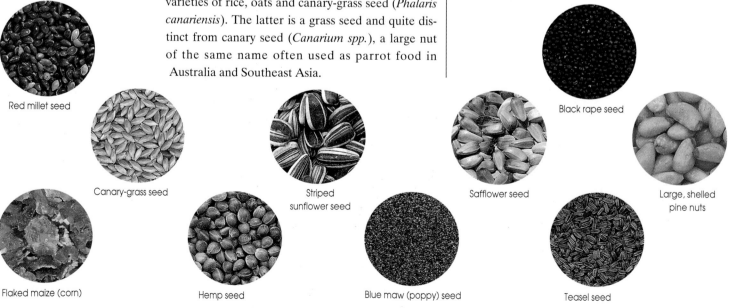

Red millet seed

Canary-grass seed

Striped sunflower seed

Safflower seed

Black rape seed

Large, shelled pine nuts

Flaked maize (corn)

Hemp seed

Blue maw (poppy) seed

Teasel seed

GREEN FOODS AND VEGETABLES

Most birds will benefit from fresh greenery. Some bird-keepers cultivate a variety of plants to ensure a year-round supply, although it is also possible to collect a diverse assortment in the wild. Be careful not to take plants from roadsides and verges, though, because of the heavy pollution and possible weed-killer treatment.

While the young seedheads of wild grasses are particularly nutritious, garden greens such as spinach and beet also make good bird food. If you are using the heads of beetroot, take care to select a strain that is low in oxalic acid. Oxalic acid is a poisonous substance and can be tolerated only in very small doses. For this reason, rhubarb leaves should never be given to birds. Cabbages should also be avoided, as they suppress thyroid activity. Lettuce, in moderation, is good, while shredded carrots help maintain the colour of plumage – they say! Watercress provides essential minerals, but should only be given in moderation. Fresh sweet corn (maize) cobs are particularly popular with parrots.

FRUIT

The growing availability of fresh tropical fruits throughout the world has made feeding birds such as the tropical softbill much easier. Tropical papaya (pawpaw), mango, watermelon and citrus can be supplemented with readily available grapes, apricots, peaches and tomatoes in more temperate regions. If fresh rambutans, lychees and similar exotic fruits become available, they should certainly be offered to your birds.

Grapes, cherries, apples, pears and most types of berry, as well as commercially available dried wild berries such as mountain ash, juniper and elderberries, are also acceptable. Birds will enjoy all types of dried fruits available for human consumption, too – soften the fruit first by soaking.

Remember that dried fruits are more concentrated, so the quantity should be reduced to about a third of the fresh quota.

In the tropics, many species of bananas flourish, while in subtropical latitudes bananas are imported and fewer varieties are available. Offer a selection of available types to establish your birds' preference and take care that the fruit is ripe yet firm, removing any pieces that are overripe or starting to decay.

Fruit should always be well washed to remove traces of insecticides and other chemical sprays, which can prove fatal to susceptible species.

When serving fruit to birds, always make sure that it is ripe and firm – and well washed to remove any traces of chemicals.

Grey-cheeked Green Pigeon.

Carrion eaters such as the Common Kestrel (Falco tinnunculus) require fresh meat in the form of dead rodents, baby chicks or even chicken heads.

MEAT

All softbills and many seed-eaters need a certain amount of animal protein, which can be supplied in the form of minced meat. Cooked chicken, beef, mutton, pork, liver and heart are all suitable. Canned dog foods can also be used, and some birds, especially parrots, will even tackle bones that have been split open to allow access to the marrow.

Larger carrion-eating birds should be fed dead rodents and baby chicks – newborn mice, known as 'pinkies', are particular favourites. It is possible to buy these foods conveniently deep-frozen and in bulk, but make sure they're thoroughly thawed out before use.

While it is true that, in the wild, animals killed by motor vehicles are quickly consumed by carrion eaters, there are sound reasons why they should never be used as a food source for aviary birds. Wild animals usually have quick reactions and avoid falling victim to vehicles; it follows that those with slow reactions may well be suffering from some disease. What appears to be a free – and interesting – roadside snack could, therefore, harbour dangerous organisms that can wipe out an entire aviary.

INVERTEBRATE FOOD

Many bird-keepers do not like handling dead chicks and rodents. Fortunately for them, these are not the only natural source of animal proteins. Invertebrates, although small and easily overlooked, are abundant in most areas and provide a diverse and highly acceptable variety of food. In addition, there are a number of invertebrates that are easy to breed (it's indeed a fascinating hobby) and that can also be purchased in bulk from pet stores and other suppliers.

Although it is more convenient to buy live invertebrate food, you can save a considerable amount by cultivating your own. This becomes particularly important when continuous supplies of live food are required, in larger quantities, for insectivorous species or during the breeding season and when young birds are reared. It is now possible to buy invertebrate cultures as well as growing containers and specially prepared invertebrate foods.

Mealworms

Mealworms

These are perhaps the most popular insect larvae food for birds. Some suppliers provide a variety of sizes, from 50mm (2in) giants to 20mm (1in) worms. Mealworms, the larvae of the Tenebrionid Beetle (*Tenebrio molitor*), are clean and easy to rear, requiring nothing more than a deep container of bran. They take about four months to reach maturity and produce another generation. The nutritional value of mealworms depends largely on what they themselves have been fed; they're low in calcium, fatty acids and certain vitamins, so their diet has to be enhanced with supplements.

Wax Moth larvae

Wax worms

Another widely used insect is the wax worm, the larva of the Wax Moth (*Galleria mellonella*). These are often fed on a rich diet of honey and wheatgerm and so provide a particularly nutritious source of food. Their soft skins make them attractive to birds.

Buffalo worms

Buffalo worms (*Alphitobius diaparinus*), the larvae of the Lesser Mealworm Beetle, are only 10–12mm (half an inch) long but provide a nutritious live food for chicks and the smaller bird species. Their rapid wriggling generates quite a lot of heat and they have a short life cycle, which makes them difficult to store.

Crickets

Many pet stores have supplies of crickets, which provide a good source of animal protein. It is necessary to buy only a small number of crickets, as they are easy to maintain and breed well in captivity. A warm, slightly moist environment is all that is needed for a life cycle completed in about six weeks. However, as adult crickets have the tendency to consume their smaller siblings, it is prudent to separate them. Newly hatched crickets are barely a millimetre in length and provide a valuable supplement to the diet of small nectar-feeders, such as sunbirds.

Crickets

Locusts

These are closely related to crickets and also easy to breed. They grow to a much bigger size – about 70mm (3in) – and are useful as food for larger birds. For both crickets and locusts, it is necessary to maintain an orderly and regular program of maintenance and propagation to ensure a continual supply. If supply outstrips demand from time to time the surplus stock can be deep-frozen for future use.

Locust

Fruit flies

For very small birds such as sunbirds and hummingbirds, fruit flies (*Drosophila*) provide a useful source of protein. Fruit flies can be attracted to and cultured on overripe bananas, but it is often better to buy a stock of vestigial-winged flies, as these escape less readily and are much less of a nuisance if they do. It is also possible to buy a yeast-rich culture medium on which fruit flies can be raised.

Ant pupae and termite larvae

Ant pupae and termite larvae are often available at local markets in the tropics.

Butterfly and moth pupae

In some places, particularly in the tropics, the pupae of large butterflies and moths are available.

Bee pupae

Bee pupae are usually more difficult to obtain, but provide a useful addition to a bird's diet. Beekeepers can harvest pupae from the comb during certain seasons and store the excess in a freezer.

Redworms and whiteworms

Redworm (*Dendrobina*) and whiteworm (*Enchytraeus*) can be placed in a small dish where they are taken by the birds as needed.

Water fleas

A very useful addition to the diets of small insectivorous birds is the common water flea (*Daphnia*). It is also fed to many types of aquarium fish.

Enteros

These tiny marine crustaceans, commonly known as backswimmers, look like small flies once they have been dried. They are a valuable addition to insectivorous food mixes.

Gammarus

Although these miniature shrimps occur in the wild throughout the world, the commercially available dried variety is usually of Southeast Asian origin. They provide another valuable source of protein in insectivorous food mixtures.

Blowfly maggots, earthworms, slugs and snails

Although blowfly maggots have been used as a valuable source of protein for birds in the past, it is now thought that they can transmit serious infections, particularly botulism. For this reason they are best avoided.

Similarly, earthworms, snails and slugs should not be used, because they commonly serve as intermediate hosts for various undesirable parasites.

Selling ants' eggs in a bird market in Indonesia.

COLOUR FEEDING

Except for parrots and their relatives, the plumage of many birds gradually loses its colour. This is partly due to dietary deficiencies and feather wear. We know that flamingos require a steady diet of small crustaceans to maintain their pink colour, but it remains a mystery why some species, such as the Green Magpie, can become blue.

So, in addition to vitamin supplements, which keep birds in top condition, other supplements are used to maintain colour.

For many years, cage birds were given carrot juice to preserve their colour through moults, because the natural carotenoids provided the necessary pigment. Today a synthetic carotenoid called Canthaxanthin is used instead. Although it is normally used just before the birds moult, many bird-keepers give small doses throughout the year without risk, as the compound is nontoxic; excessive doses merely result in brightly coloured droppings.

WATER

Birds should always have access to clean drinking water – it should never be allowed to become contaminated, so should be placed in a covered area (if in an aviary) or in a drinking hopper (if in a cage). Where ground-based hoppers are unavoidable, as with many ground-living species, they should be easily accessible, and cleaned and refilled regularly. Since birds cannot differentiate between bathing and drinking facilities, cleanliness is equally important for bathing water.

During cold weather in temperate climates, drinking water needs special attention. Regular refilling with tepid water is one possibility, which can be made less of a chore if the feeding area is sheltered or indoors. Some bird-keepers add about 10 per cent sugar or 20 per cent honey to the water to inhibit fast freezing. While this is nutritious, it should not be offered more than once a week or allowed to go stale. Great care must also be taken to prevent the birds from bathing in it.

ABOVE A large water dispenser and, RIGHT, a ground-level water hopper keep drinking water free of contaminants and prevent the birds from bathing in it.

FEEDING GUIDELINES

In order to plan the appropriate diets for your birds it is essential to understand the needs of individual species and take into account the ways in which they are kept and housed. Aviary birds, for instance, get more exercise and expend more energy than cage birds. They are also exposed to climatic changes, both seasonal and diurnal. Cage birds, on the other hand, are consequently less demanding and can survive on a much lighter diet.

SEED DIETS

For the novice, the available choice of prepacked seed mixtures can be quite bewildering. Most include similar basic constituents with added supplements to suit the needs of a particular bird type. Seed mixtures can lead to wastage when birds refuse to eat certain of the seeds offered – this can be remedied by determining which seed is shunned and then preparing your own mix. As a guide to quantity, small, active seed-eaters consume 6–8g (about a quarter of an ounce) of seed a day, but you must also allow for wastage.

Listed below is a suggested variety of seed mixtures for the main bird groups. These diets have been well proven by bird-keepers in the more temperate regions such as Europe and the US and may need to be modified slightly for tropical conditions. They have been formulated to meet certain needs and provide a good balance of fat, carbohydrate, protein as well as many of the essential vitamins and minerals.

The list is not exhaustive, though, and other mixtures may be just as good. In some countries, hemp is illegal, and these seeds must be replaced by others. Remember that variety is essential and that most seed-eaters will also consume some insect and green food; others will occasionally eat fruit and berries. Certain minerals and grit must always be provided along with the seed.

Seed Mixture 1: Aviary-housed canaries
The high calorie content of this diet provides balanced high-energy nourishment for well-exercised birds such as canaries kept in aviaries, including Type as well as Coloured canaries. Singing canaries like Rollers and American Singers may also be kept in aviaries outside the breeding season and could then be given the same diet. When they are brought

indoors into cages in the late autumn, however, the diet needs to be modified slightly. Indoors they will get less exercise, so to prevent them from getting fat, their diet will need to be modified slightly: fat birds simply do not sing.

Seed Mixture 2: Caged canaries
Caged canaries are invariably kept for their song, so must be fed a diet that is low in carbohydrates to keep them fit without getting too fat (see above).

Seed Mixture 3: Small tropical finches
This seed mixture is suitable for small, active finches including Bengalese and Zebra Finches, as well as waxbills, some of the smaller munias and grass-finches. These are normally kept in aviaries where they expend a lot of energy and so require considerable amounts of carbohydrate. Tropical seed-eaters normally consume diverse seed species and, while it is impossible to mirror this diet in captivity, variety should be offered in the form of small daily supplements consisting of seeds, live and green food. They will also enjoy millet sprays suspended in the aviary.

Seed Mixture 4: Large tropical finches
Large tropical finches, such as Java Sparrows, weavers and whydahs, the buntings, cardinals, doves and quails, can also be given a similar seed diet, with the addition of larger grains such as sunflower or safflower. Additions of live and green foods and supplementary seeds, as described for the small tropical finches, should also be offered.

For ground-feeding birds, such as quails and doves, supplementary seed should be scattered over the aviary floor to encourage their natural foraging habits. The larger species could also benefit from small additions of broken wheat and buckwheat.

Seed Mixture 5: Small parrotlike birds
Budgerigars and lovebirds are more delicate eaters and require a seed mixture slightly different to that of the larger parrots. In addition to the basic mixture, they also benefit from small daily supplements of aniseed, linseed, Niger seed, teasel seed, pine nuts and rape, safflower, sesame, wheat and maize seed. Fresh green food and fruit supply essential minerals and vitamins, while cuttlefish bone provides calcium for bones. Millet sprays encourage foraging habits.

Seed Mixture 6: Large parrotlike birds
Cockatiels, Australian parakeets, rosellas and conures require a similar diet to that of the smaller parrot-like birds, but with the addition of sunflower seed. Daily supplements of other seeds should be offered as suggested for the small, parrot-like birds above. A few fresh peanuts and hemp seeds can be offered occasionally.

Seed Mixture 7: Parrots
Parrots may exist for ages on nothing but sunflower seeds and water, but peak health is only maintained through a varied and balanced diet. Sickness in parrots is often due to inappropriate feeding. Parrots habitually pick out the sunflower seeds first, before they turn to any other offerings.

SEED MIXTURE	1	2	3	4	5	6	7
	(%)	(%)	(%)	(%)	(%)	(%)	(%)
canary grass	30	35	15	20	30	25	10
white millet	5	-	25	20	15	15	10
yellow millet	15	-	35	40	20	15	-
red millet	5	-	15	-	15	15	-
broken oats	5	4	-	2	10	10	5
red rape	25	55	5	5	1	1	-
linseed	3	1	1	2	1	1	-
hemp	3	-	1	-	-	-	-
Niger seed (ramtil)	5	3	-	2	1	1	5
maw (poppy)	4	1	1	1	1	1	-
sunflower	-	-	-	2	-	10	25
safflower	-	-	-	-	1	1	-
teasel	-	1	1	2	2	2	-
sesame	-	-	1	2	1	1	-
aniseed	-	-	-	2	2	2	-
walnuts (shelled)	-	-	-	-	-	-	10
Brazil nuts (shelled)	-	-	-	-	-	-	10
peanuts (in or out of shell)	-	-	-	-	-	-	10
flaked maize or cracked corn	-	-	-	-	-	-	5
dried dog pellets	-	-	-	-	-	-	10
FOOD VALUE							
(%) FAT	18	26	7	7	7	7	20
(%) CARBOHYDRATE	39	30	60	55	60	55	55
(%) PROTEIN	16	20	13	13	13	14	16

Supplementary seeds

Birds invariably choose supplementary seeds over their basic diet, eating them to excess if allowed; offer supplementary seeds in small, daily quantities. Ideally, separate containers should be used so that preferences can be monitored and a balanced diet maintained. Excessive intake of supplementary seeds can lead to obesity, especially in the larger and less active tropical seed-eaters such as quails and doves. Useful supplements include aniseed, linseed and hemp, maw (poppy), Niger (ramtil), oats, sesame, safflower, sunflower and teasel seeds.

Soaked seed

Seeds can be particularly beneficial when soaked, as long as suitable precautions are taken to prevent the growth of mould. Leaving the seed in warm water overnight makes them more digestible and raises their protein content. It must be emphasized, though, that they should not be allowed to soak for too long as this could lead to fermentation, leading to illnesses such as crop-swelling. The secret is to prepare only enough for a single feed and not leave leftovers lying about.

In addition to conventional bird seeds, pulses like beans also make useful additions to the diet. It is very important that soaked pulses be washed very thoroughly before they are offered as food in order to remove traces of mould and impurities.

Seed for soaking

Germinated seed

Most birds enjoy germinated seeds, which provide a rich source of vitamins A and E. Presoaking in luke-warm water for about half a day is necessary to con-vert starch into dextrin, a form of sugar. Thoroughly rinse the seed in clean water before allowing it to drain, then keep it covered with a damp cloth in a warm place. Regular rinsing and draining every few hours will discourage fermentation and the growth of mould. After 24 hours the seed should start to germinate and be ready for the birds.

Finches and canaries relish germinated seed, but offer it only in small quantities, as a supplement mixed with the main diet. Germinated seed is also important during the rearing of chicks when it can be used instead of commercial rearing foods. Offer only in small quantities, otherwise parent birds will feed their chicks nothing but germinated seed.

Germinated seed

FRUIT AND VEGETABLE PREPARATION

Besides frugiverous birds, many others, including some seed-eaters, will eat fruit and vegetables, if they're offered them. To ensure a well-balanced diet, offer fresh fruit every day.

Wash the fruit well and chop it into cubes appro-priate to the size of the birds – this prevents the soiling of the head feathers, particularly among species such as fruit doves.

Serve most of the fruit in a bowl to ensure variety. To encourage natural foraging habits in aviaries, large pieces of fruit like banana, orange or papaya may also be hung on hooks at a fixed feeding station.

Fruit must not become stale or soiled by drop-pings, so it is essential to change it regularly and clean the area around the feeding station of scat-tered food debris.

Vegetables and greenstuff can be chopped finely and mixed with fruit, but for seed-eaters greens can be suspended in convenient bunches where they will not get soiled. Serve the greens very fresh and remove them as soon as they begin to wilt.

COMMERCIAL FOOD PREPARATIONS
Pellets

In many parts of the world, pellet food has been developed for the poultry industry and subsequently refined and rebalanced to provide an excellent diet for cage and aviary birds. Fruit powders and dried insects are often added, and the small pellets are suitable for even the tiniest of beaks. Various types have been formulated to create complete balanced diets for several groups of birds, including poultry, pheasants, mynahs, parrots and chicks.

Pellets

Softbill foods

There are many excellent proprietary brands of ready prepared soft foods available for a wide range of species. Although many enthusiasts prefer to create their own special food blends, this is time consuming and not really necessary. Although sold primarily for softbills, the high-protein mixes will also benefit seed-eaters during breeding.

The composition of soft foods varies between manufacturers, but in general they consist of fruit, berries, fresh-water shrimps, sugar and honey, yeast, cereals, seeds, vegetables and fish, fortified with minerals and vitamins. They ensure a good, balanced diet and are a convenient way to feed softbills, but it is essential to offer only the recommended daily requirement to ensure a fresh ration each day. Proprietary soft foods can deteriorate in storage, so ensure that your supplier gets fresh stock regularly.

Fruit-based soft foods contain essentially the same constituents as the universal soft foods but the proportion of fruit is increased considerably. Fruit pieces are added in the form of chopped figs, apricots, papaya, pineapple and berries. Insectile soft foods contain as much as 30 per cent dried insects, as well as gammarus shrimps, egg, cereals, seeds, vegetables, sugar and honey, plus vitamins and minerals.

Some soft foods are designed to be mixed with water to form a gruel, while others are intended to be eaten dry and come in a variety of sizes. Birds tend to become used to a particular form. Although variety is good, the transition from one to another should always be gradual. Many bird-keepers simply sprinkle soft food mixture onto the regular food, while others provide it in a separate dish.

Bogena softbill food

EGG AND REARING FOODS

Commercial egg and rearing foods are a convenient diet for newly hatched chicks, although it is common practice for breeders to concoct their own egg foods to stimulate healthy growth in young birds and support the breeding adults. It is essential that the birds receive no more than the essential types and quantities of vitamins. Many young birds have been lost due to overfeeding. This type of food needs to be offered fresh and should be removed before it turns sour.

It is easy to prepare your own egg and rearing food. Make a small omelette with a beaten fresh chicken's egg to which half a teaspoon of margarine has been added. When cool, chop it into small pieces and add four small babies' rusks broken into crumbs. Mix in a quarter of finely diced or grated sweet apple or pear, along with a tablespoon of fresh orange juice. Do not let the mixture become stale.

Another useful and very simple recipe uses bread and milk. Soak a slice of stale white or brown bread in clean water until it is soggy, then squeeze out the excess liquid. Mix in a little fresh milk to form a porridge consistency. This can be fed to all birds and is especially relished by tropical species. Use no more than twice a week to maintain variety. Do not allow the mixture to become sour, and remove it after a few hours.

Egg biscuit food

Nectar

There are many nectar substitutes, each formulated to meet the needs of a specific group of birds. They vary in carbohydrate and protein content (excessive protein is linked to gout). However, many bird-keepers prefer to mix their own formulations, combining sugar or honey with pollen granules and even human food supplements.

It should be remembered that solutions rich in sugars provide a perfect breeding ground for yeasts. For this reason, even if yeast suppressants are added, the mixture should be replaced in clean containers every 24 hours.

A note of warning: many nectar-feeders, particularly lories and hanging parrots, are sensitive to sudden changes in their diet. The penalty for failing to allow a gradual diet transition can be an attack of enterotoxemia, a rapidly fatal disorder of the gut. Also, remember that nectar mixtures are no substitute for fresh drinking water, which should always be available separately and kept covered and free from contamination.

Nectar blend rearing food

THE COLLOIDAL SILVER GENERATOR
THE PATHOGEN KILLER

Prior to the advent of antibiotics, it was common to use colloidal silver to remove bacterial, viral and fungal infections. For example, practices such as bathing one's feet in it to clear athletes foot and using a silver dollar in milk to preserve it were common in the 1930s. Pigeon fanciers have proven that colloidal silver is particularly effective; and what group of birds are more prone to nasty bugs than pigeons!

Recent technology has allowed the development of a very simple little device that will easily generate colloidal silver just by immersing its silver electrodes into a container of clean water. Originally designed for use in the preparation of an elementary human 'antibiotic', it is equally useful for cage and aviary birds.

Limestone grit

Oystershell grit

Mineral grit

BELOW An iodized conditioning block to help prevent goitres.

ABOVE Cuttlefish bone provides calcium and phosphorus.
OPPOSITE These macaws, here eating seed, also enjoy green food.

ADDITIONAL DIETARY NEEDS
Grit
During the first stage of the digestive process, the nutritious inner parts of the seeds are exposed to enzymes that will break them down into chemical compounds. This takes place in the acid environment of the bird's gizzard, and is assisted by small stones that the seed-eater takes in with its food. Birds are often seen pecking gravel by the roadside. For captive birds, these stones, or grit, must be provided by the bird-keeper.

Grit falls into two categories: the hard, indigestible flinty bits that remain within the gizzard for quite a long time, and the more soluble particles composed of calcium carbonate (such as that from cuttlefish bone) or limestone that contribute minerals necessary for bone and eggshell formation. Grit is available in various grades and can be chosen according to the size of the bird.

Iodine nibbles
Some birds, notably budgerigars, are prone to goitres (see p76). This condition is caused by enlarged thyroid glands, and indicates an iodine deficiency. Many seed and cuttlebone suppliers also stock iodine nibbles (or conditioning pecks, as they are sometimes called). They incorporate calcium, yeast, kelp, grits and iodine.

Cuttlefish bone, the internal skeleton of a kind of squid, has long been used to supplement the diet of seed-eaters. It provides a valuable source of calcium and phosphorus.

Cuttlefish bones are washed up on beaches around the world, sometimes reaching 45cm (17in) in length. If you collect them yourself, be sure they are not contaminated with oil. They should be soaked for several days and scrubbed thoroughly before being dried in the oven. Once dried, cuttlefish bones last indefinitely, but if they are dirtied by droppings or are walked over, regular scrubbing is essential to keep them clean. Some small birds find it hard to break pieces off a large cuttlefish bone, so you could provide small, broken fragments in a suitable dish.

Hens are particularly dependent on dietary calcium during the breeding season and young birds require it for development. Cuttlefish bone may not be sufficient at these critical times, and supplements, now used regularly throughout the year for non-breeding birds too, are a good way of providing additional calcium. Several brands are available.

HEALTH, HYGIENE AND WELL-BEING

PREVIOUS PAGES These Monk Parakeets (Myiopsitta monarchus) *and Indian ring-necked Parakeets (*Psittacula krameri*) make up an exceptionally noisy colony.*

Most birds will thrive in captivity, provided they are properly fed and kept in clean surroundings, free from stress and exposure to disease. However, changes in accustomed diet and the stress of being moved or disturbed, and the introduction of new birds, can lead to disease.

Bird-keepers must always be alert to early signs of trouble and recognize when professional help is needed. Fortunately, avian medicine has benefited from the progress made in the control of human disease. This is particularly true for bacterial infections, which can now largely be controlled with antibiotics. Viral infections, for the most part, still remain a serious, unresolved problem.

PREVENTION OF DISEASE

Prevention is always better than cure. In general, ill health in cage and aviary birds can be traced directly to poor hygiene, so careful attention to basic management practices and cleanliness will greatly reduce the risk. As a rule, bird-keepers ought to wash their hands thoroughly before and after handling stock, for their own benefit and for that of their birds. If you suspect illness among your birds, wash even more assiduously, using a strong disinfectant.

Most disorders are spread through direct and indirect contact with other birds. Hence, it is important to prevent droppings of wild birds (and vermin)

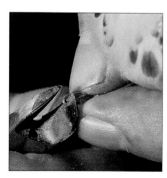

ABOVE A budgerigar submits to a necessary pedicure.
*TOP A Monk Parakeet (*Myiopsitta monarchus*) preening.*

from contaminating outdoor aviaries or flights by protecting at least the feeding, watering and bathing areas with a waterproof covering on the top of the aviary. Likewise, old droppings left in a cage by a previous occupant can be a source of contamination.

A further risk of infection is presented by people who have been in contact with sick birds. This is a particular problem with members of the parrot family, which are highly susceptible to Psittacine Bill (beak) and Feather Disease (PBFD). Specialists who hand-rear young birds often unwittingly spread the disease, because they are continually in contact with

Blue-and-Yellow Macaws (Ara ararauna) *– noisy, hardy birds – do well in small groups in large aviaries.*

many different birds. The moral here is to do your own hand-rearing – although it is almost as demanding as raising a human infant, it can be as rewarding.

QUARANTINE

Quarantine should be routine practice. New birds must always be isolated for at least two weeks or more, to prevent the spread of disease as well as to allow them to settle in without being bullied by established stock. New birds should be closely monitored at least twice a day for evidence of illness. Warning signs include loss of appetite, discoloration of feathers around the vent, wet, laboured breathing and a general lack of vitality, often accompanied by a fluffing up of the plumage, sleeping and a change in droppings. Remember also that the first moult, which varies from species to species, is a critical period (particularly for softbills), so be extra vigilant.

Although most imported birds will have undergone enforced governmental quarantine to prevent the spread of specific foreign diseases, they're not necessarily free of all infection. While in transit, they may have picked up an illness that was not monitored during quarantine.

ABOVE *This Speckled Mouse-bird* (Colius striatus), *despite its overgrown beak, is able to fend for itself in a peaceful aviary.*
RIGHT *A typical, commercially produced hospital cage.*
OPPOSITE BELOW *Vets treating a sick parrot.*

STRESS

Stress is a complicated problem in birds. Although its full effects are unclear, it is known that stressed birds are more likely to be affected by eating disorders and succumb to infection. Other catastrophic effects range from the disturbance of breeding birds and a resultant loss of their young to injuries sustained by flying into objects when frightened.

Cats rank high on the list of potential trouble, so you may need to control the family pet. Squirrels, snakes, rodents and other natural predators can also cause havoc. Keeping pests at bay can be an ongoing challenge, but certain precautions can be taken (see p51).

Another form of disturbance may be encountered within the aviary environment itself: some normally passive species can become extremely territorial and aggressive while breeding. Troublemakers must be isolated at the first sign of commotion.

'Moving house' is also very stressful for birds, so make sure your birds are in peak condition to withstand the trauma. At no time is this more important than when birds are entered for competition (although no wise keeper would even consider entering an unfit bird). Diet, naturally, plays an important part in preparation for a move, and there are also several commercial food additives, such as probiotics (see p82), that help birds cope with stress.

CARE OF SICK BIRDS

When you suspect a bird is unwell, take immediate action. It must be isolated from other stock and kept warm. Ideally, it should be transferred to a special hospital cage, but improvized accommodation such as a well-ventilated, closed cardboard box placed in a warm cupboard is acceptable in emergency situations. Heating can be provided by a small (40W) light bulb placed at least 60cm (23in) below the box; remove any combustible material in the vicinity and ensure that the bird is not overheated. Keeping the patient in the dark allows it to relax and sleep.

Some bird-keepers prefer to construct more permanent accommodation. In this case, ceramic heaters should be used in preference to light bulbs – unfortunately the glass bulbs shatter if they are splashed with water.

THE HOSPITAL CAGE

A hospital cage, which can be purchased complete, should be small but not cramped. If you keep birds of different sizes, choose a hospital cage in which the largest bird will fit comfortably. Smaller birds can then be confined by constructing a makeshift nest with a towel or piece of soft cloth. The enclosure

should have adequate but draught-free ventilation and allow the bird easy access to food and water. It should also afford a clear view of the patient, allow easy access for handling and be equipped with thermostatically controlled infrared heating; a conspicuous external thermometer makes it easy to monitor the temperature. The cage should be constructed in a way that facilitates easy disinfection and sterilization between uses.

Infra-red lamp

Owing to their more rapid metabolism, birds normally maintain a higher body temperature than humans. Because a sick bird doesn't feed properly, its metabolic rate and temperature drop. Death through hypothermia then becomes a real danger, so a hospital cage should be carefully maintained at about 30° C (86° F).

Once the patient begins to recover, treat it sensitively and allow ample time for recuperation. Reduce the temperature of the cage gradually to allow the bird to readjust. It goes without saying that a bird recently recovered from an illness should not immediately be returned to the company of other birds; neither should it be placed in an outdoor aviary where temperature variations can be considerable.

EXPERT OPINION

Many common avian diseases can be recognized and treated without consulting a veterinary specialist. However, if there is any doubt about the correctness of a diagnosis, if several birds are afflicted or if one has died, do seek expert opinion. In many countries veterinary prescriptions are needed for sulphonamides, antibiotics and other drugs.

Remember that most bacterial infections can be treated quickly with the proper antibiotics, while fungal and viral infections do not respond well to treatment. Sick birds deteriorate rapidly so it is quite common for a vet to prescribe broad-spectrum antibiotics at the first sign of illness. Once laboratory specimens have been analyzed, the treatment can be changed accordingly. Prescribed drugs must be applied exactly as instructed by the vet.

BIRD-KEEPERS' FIRST-AID KIT

Keep a small stock of medical necessities for your birds, particularly if there is no vet nearby. Ensure that all medicines are kept sealed in a locked container, out of the reach of children. All equipment should be cleaned and disinfected after use and stored so that it remains clean. Ensure that drugs are within their 'use-by' date and have been stored as recommended. Destroy any expired drugs.

EQUIPMENT
Nail clippers (the proper side-cutting type)
Forceps
Disposable plastic cups for washing wounds, feet, etc
Paper towels
Cotton buds and small, soft artists' paint brush for applying oil or antiseptic medication
Gauze bandages and sticky plaster (for holding bandages)
Crop tubes (sizes to suit the birds)

MEDICATION
Antiseptic ointment
Red-mite spray (Johnson's Anti-mite)
Dioralyte and Glucose powder for rehydrating
Styptic pencil or alum powder for stopping minor bleeding
Olive oil or petroleum jelly (Vaseline) to relieve egg-binding
Eye ointments or drops
Powdered aloe to stop feather plucking
Disinfectant

Veterinary assistance may also be necessary to administer certain medications. Most seed-eaters can be treated by impregnating their food with drugs. In some cases, medication can also be dissolved in the drinking water. Nectar-feeders, however, react strongly to the bitter taste and it may be necessary to resort to injections, or passing a tube down into the bird's crop to administer liquid medicine internally. The latter techniques are also called for when precise dosages are required.

As a rule, always wash your hands thoroughly with a strong disinfectant solution after handling ill birds or their surroundings. Remember that even after a bird is seemingly cured, its gut may still contain infectious organisms for some time, which can spread to other birds and their handlers.

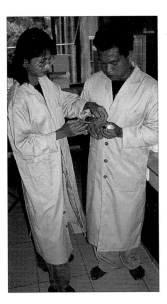

RECOGNITION AND TREATMENT OF COMMON BIRD AILMENTS

AREA	SYMPTOM	DIAGNOSIS	PROBABLE CAUSE	TREATMENT
RESPIRATORY TRACT	Excessive movement of the tail due to laboured breathing; tail bobbing	Sinus infection	Fungal nasal infection; underlying vitamin A deficiency	Clear the nostrils of fluid discharge and blockage by washing gently (best done by a vet), followed by the administration of decongestants. (Sinus infections often prove resistant to treatment and frequently return.) Anti-fungal treatment.
	Breathing problems and an enlarged thyroid	A goitre that exerts pressure on the trachea	A low-iodine diet (particularly a problem with budgerigars)	Make sure your birds have a regular supply of supplementary iodine and consult a vet.
	Wheezing and breathing difficulty after flight; voice change or loss; coughing and gasping	Tracheal mites (canaries and finches) or gapeworm infection (larger, gallinaceous birds)	Mites transferred by adults during feeding; worms through hosts such as earthworms	Treat with the drug Ivermectin, which is absorbed through the skin (a few drops on the neck of small birds or an intramuscular injection).
	Breathing difficulties and some diarrhoea (and few other symptoms)	Pasturella, an infection that strikes swiftly and fatally, particularly in young birds	This serious bacterial infection is transmitted by rodents and wild birds.	Prompt administration of antibiotics often leads to a full recovery.
	No apparent symptoms; or breathing difficulties that are unresponsive to antibiotics	Aspergillosis, the most common and very serious fungal infection of the respiratory tract (psittacines and raptors are particularly susceptible to attack)	Crowded, ill-ventilated conditions, particularly where humidity is high; malnutrition caused by immuno-suppression	There is no known cure, although the human drug ketoconazole (Nizoral) can sometimes help. Infected birds usually cannot be isolated early enough and the disease spreads rapidly. If the infection is recognized, scrub the aviary and surrounds with strong washing soda (sodium carbonate) or another suitable disinfectant. All surviving birds must be isolated from each other and treated as advised by the vet. Disinfect and wash everything between patients.
	Cold-like symptoms with dripping nostrils and breathing difficulties; enteritis may also be present and the bird will appear exhausted; eye trouble	Psittacosis (Ornithosis); for years this disease resulted in a widespread ban on the trade in parrots; it can affect a wide range of animals, as well as humans, and can lead to pneumonia and death	Infection (Clamydia), common in psittacines	Treat with antibiotics (Doxycycline).
	Lethargy and progressive weight loss	Avian tuberculosis; can also be passed on to humans	Crowded, humid conditions; low immunity	Seek veterinary advice; treatment is available but a cure is not guaranteed.

RECOGNITION AND TREATMENT OF COMMON BIRD AILMENTS

AREA	SYMPTOM	DIAGNOSIS	PROBABLE CAUSE	TREATMENT
DIGESTIVE TRACT	Bloody diarrhoea, paralysis of the legs and muscular twitching	Fowl Pest (also known as Newcastle Disease), more prominent in poultry but also known to affect other birds, especially psittacines	A virus often spread by wild birds	No known treatment. Fortunately, it is rare where stringent quarantine laws are applied, and where all affected birds, together with any that may have been in contact with them, are slaughtered. Fowl Pest is one of the main reasons for the strict governmental quarantine restrictions on the movement of birds. Many countries seem to have a local strain of this virus. In the Indonesian archipelago, for example, each island appears to have its own local variant to which native birds have acquired resistance. However, when birds are taken to other islands, they frequently succumb to a different strain.
	The term 'enteritis' is often used for gut ailments, but applied indiscriminately to refer to any unusual condition of the droppings. Diarrhoea may be no more than a sensitive reaction to a change in the accustomed diet, but bird-keepers should learn to recognize more serious conditions. If the problem is persistent, veterinary advice should be obtained. As a rule, always wash your hands thoroughly with strong disinfectant solution after handling ill birds or their surroundings. Remember that even after a bird is seemingly cured, its gut may still contain infectious organisms for some time, which can spread to other birds and their handlers.			
	Lethargy and exhaustion, accompanied by fluffed-up plumage	'Going Light' Syndrome – weight loss (occurs mainly in juvenile birds that have recently fledged, or adults that have undergone a difficult moult)	Many different causes, but often weight loss is caused by stress or illness	If diagnosed early, the use of probiotics fed by crop-tube may save the bird from almost certain death. Sick birds, especially those suffering from enteritis, rapidly become dehydrated, and the use of the crop-tube to administer fluids can be equally as important as the medication itself.
	Lethargy, stained feathers around the vent (cloaca) and a huddled posture	Salmonella poisoning (transmissible, and possibly fatal, to humans)	Dirty conditions, rodent droppings or the feeding of contaminated foods	The bacterium responds well to antibiotics and birds soon improve with care and attention.
	Mild lethargy and progressive weight loss	Pseudotuberculosis (tanagers and other softbills appear very prone to it)	Spread through droppings, and difficult to control	No known cure, although cleanliness and prevention of contamination from wild bird droppings will help to avoid it.
	Paralysis of the respiratory and cardiac muscles	Botulism (also known as Limberneck)	Feeding with improperly cleansed maggots that have fed on putrid meat	Death results within a few hours of ingestion; keepers with rapid access to an antitoxin may be able to save their birds.
	Birds sitting with their bills open and tongue extended; in bad cases, a creamy white fungus coating the inside of the bill	Candidiasis Fungus (common in lorikeets and other nectar-feeders)	A vitamin A deficiency	Apply antibiotics directly to the affected area and offer vitamin A supplements.
	Excess mucous production, retching and vomiting a bubbly froth (often results in stained head feathers)	Sour Crop (common in budgerigars), associated with candida	A protozoan parasite	Hold the bird upside down and massage the secretions out of its crop; Dimetridazol provides a reliable cure.

RECOGNITION AND TREATMENT OF COMMON BIRD AILMENTS

AREA	SYMPTOM	DIAGNOSIS	PROBABLE CAUSE	TREATMENT
REPRODUCTIVE SYSTEM	The egg fails to pass through the reproductive tract, causing a blockage.	Egg-binding	A mineral imbalance resulting from calcium deficiency	Apply lubricant, or consult a vet.
	Small warts around or on the cloaca	Papillomas (warts); distinguishable from a prolapse by their bleeding; highly contagious and common in macaws and Amazon parrots. They can cause severe obstruction of the cloaca, resulting in constipation; mating is physically impossible	The cause has not been identified with certainty	Bathe the affected areas with a silver nitrate solution, which shrinks the papillomas within a few days. Once a bird has been cured and has not suffered a relapse for 12 months, it may safely be allowed to mate without fear of transmitting the disease.
	Swellings and lesions around the face and legs	Avian pox; the lesions may burst and infect other birds	A viral infection spread by mosquitoes, particularly near marshy areas in the more tropical climates	No effective treatment, although a vaccine is available. Good hygiene will aid prevention; some breeders protect their aviaries with mosquito netting.
FEATHERS	Loss of primary flight feathers and tail feathers, often accompanied by bleeding; severely irregular and often distorted plumage	French moult, the most common feather disorder, which often afflicts young budgerigars, lovebirds, macaws, cockatiels and Ring-necked Parakeets. Some attacks are so severe that the bird never recovers its ability to fly.	A virus and poor diet	No known remedy, but the disease is rarely fatal and replacement feathers often develop normally and show no signs of disease. Even in cases that appear cured, there remains the very real possibility that the virus is still present and active, so take care to prevent contact with breeding stock.
	Feathers, claws and bill look 'diseased'.	A viral infection	Feather Maturation Syndrome (feather rot), common in cockatoos	The only course of action is prevention, with isolation, scrupulous cleanliness and close attention to hygiene; some breeders maintain that the use of an ionizer in the bird room is beneficial in destroying airborne viruses.
	The gradual distortion and increasing fragility of feathers; a softening of the bill and claws	Psittacine Bill (Beak) and Feather Disease (PBFD), also known as Budgerigar Fledgling Disease; usually fatal	A viral disease associated with inadequate thyroid gland secretions	No known cure; thyroid hormones, administered by a vet, offer some relief.
	Lumps on the feathers	Feather cysts	Caused when the feathers become too bulky through inbreeding – common in canaries	A genetic problem for which there is no known cure

RECOGNITION AND TREATMENT OF COMMON BIRD AILMENTS

AREA	SYMPTOM	DIAGNOSIS	PROBABLE CAUSE	TREATMENT
EYES	Eye trouble	Eye infections – rarely serious. It could also indicate psittacosis (see p76).	Infections caused by abrasions and rubbing *This Plum-headed Parakeet has an eye injury, which led to an infection.*	Treat with ophthalmic ointments or drops. Drops leave no residue on the feathers but tend to be washed away by the natural eye secretions, so a carefully applied cream is generally more effective. Affected birds tend to rub their eyes on the perch, so take care to thoroughly disinfect the perches regularly.
FEET AND BILLS	Swellings on the toe joints	Bumblefoot	Bacterial infections that originate from small cuts in the skin; minor wounds caused by splinters, sharp wires or frostbite can become infected with staphylococci, particularly where droppings have accumulated on perches or the cage floor.	Treat promptly with antibiotics; if the condition is allowed to deteriorate, surgery may be the only effective cure. If left untreated, blood flow to the limb may become compromised, eventually leading to gangrene and loss of the foot.
	Hard lumps on the toes	Gout (may be confused with bumblefoot, but has a slower onset)	The build-up of crystalline deposits in the joints, which can ultimately lead to the loss of toes and feet. Common in hummingbirds fed on a high-protein diet and in older birds suffering from failing kidneys; the kidneys are unable to remove the toxic metabolic by-products fast enough, which are then deposited in the tissues.	No known treatment
	Calluses		Caused by hard perches of uniform diameter; poor conditions	Provide a variety of natural perches in different sizes.
	Long, irregular claws	Common among finches	Lack of wear due to regular shaped, smooth perches	Clip the offending claws regularly, taking care not to cut too far back into the blood vessels. The blood supply to back claws can be particularly difficult to locate, so extra care is necessary. Dab the claw with a styptic pencil if it starts to bleed.
	Overgrown, malformed bills, which make feeding difficult	Uncommon; more common in budgerigars	Poor nest hygiene may cause undershot bills; insufficient wear may cause overshot bills (such as in this budgerigar).	If in doubt about the cause, consult a vet. LEFT *A cockatiel with an overgrown upper mandible, curving right down under the lower mandible.*

EGG-BINDING

Egg-binding is a distressing condition that occurs most frequently in young female birds, often during cold weather. The egg fails to pass through the reproductive tract and causes a blockage.

The cause is not wholly understood, but appears to be associated with a mineral imbalance resulting from calcium deficiency and the inability of the female to expel the egg by muscle contraction.

It is sometimes possible to ease the egg out with a little lubricant such as warmed olive oil or petroleum jelly (Vaseline). Warming the bird to about 32°C (89°F) in a hospital cage for a few hours can also help.

Take great care not to break the egg within the hen's body as this can cause peritonitis, an inflammation of the abdominal cavity that is usually fatal. Rather seek veterinary assistance, either for an injection of calcium borogluconate or surgery. In any event, speed is essential if the hen is to be saved.

If the afflicted bird survives the ordeal it will require prolonged convalescence and reacclimatization. Although egg-binding is not confined to mated hens and may occur in solitary birds, recovering individuals should not be allowed to breed for at least four months – preferably not until the following season.

Prolonged egg-binding can sometimes result in cloacal prolapse, a sort of avian haemorrhoid. This pinkish protrusion from the vent can usually be pushed back quite easily, particularly if a little lubricant is applied. If the bird has continuing difficulty holding in the prolapse, you may need a vet to secure it in place with a temporary suture.

ENDOPARASITES

Roundworms and tapeworms

Birds play host to a wide variety of internal and external parasites. Among the former are numerous roundworms, tape worms and a large variety of protozoans.

Roundworm and tapeworm infestations are common in softbills and psittacines, but are usually only life-threatening when present in large numbers. Today they can be controlled quite easily with a number of proprietary avermectin drugs, some of which are also effective for getting rid of air-sac mites (*sternostoma*), which are hard to eradicate by other means.

Nematode roundworms and tapeworms are often spread in exposed outdoor aviaries through the droppings of wild birds, and are a particular problem with parakeets and cockatiels. Since they are intestinal parasites, their eggs pass out with the birds' droppings. The problem is exacerbated if the floor of the aviary is grassed over – ideal conditions for roundworms to flourish and spread. Ground-feeding birds are all too easy reinfected.

The large lumps of dirt attached to the foot of this Japanese Quail (Coturnix japonica) *have accumulated through a damp and unclean aviary floor.*

Protozoans

Coccidae

The most common protozoan pest is coccidae, which cause the bird to have bloody diarrhoea. Infection is not serious and can be readily treated with sulpha drugs.

Leucocytozoon

Leucocytozoon is transmitted by a variety of invertebrates, including mites and biting flies. It is always fatal and precautions are necessary to avoid it. In high-risk areas, this may mean protecting the cages or aviaries with mosquito netting for the appropriate season and maintaining a clean environment inimical to mites. Various aviary insecticides are available for this purpose.

Leucocytozoon forms cysts in the heart muscle and can cause sudden death. Its presence can only be detected by microscopic examination of blood samples, so if a bird dies unexpectedly the body should be kept for a postmortem examination by a veterinary surgeon.

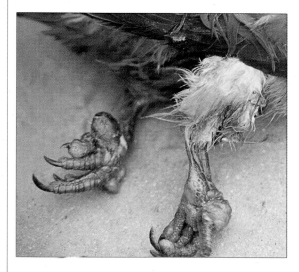

A bad case of Avian Pox (pocks). The pustules are highly contagious and are easily transmitted on contact – they are usually caused by mosquito bites.

Lankesterella

Another fatal protozoan is Lankesterella, which can be carried by red mite (*Dermanyssus gallinae*), and attacks the white blood cells. Apart from general lethargy there are no obvious symptoms.

ECTOPARASITES

Red mites

Of the external parasites, red mites are, perhaps, the most common. In themselves, red mites are not serious pests and can easily be controlled with special sprays, powders and washes.

Because they suck the blood of birds, which gives them their red colouring, they can cause anaemia in the young. Much of their life cycle is spent in nest boxes and other dark areas. Consequently their elimination requires extensive treatment of bird rooms, aviaries and their furnishings – use proprietary sprays, washes or powders.

Biting and sucking lice

The biting lice found on birds belong to the order *Mallophaga* and are quite distinct from the sucking lice (*Anoplura*) occurring on humans and other mammals. Bird lice live on their hosts permanently, feeding on feathers and skin debris. Although irritating, they do not appear to do serious harm. Insecticide sprays and washes as used for red mite may help to eliminate them.

Scaly-face mites

The most conspicuous parasites found on birds are scaly-face mites (*Knemidocoptes pilae*), common on members of the parrot family, especially budgerigars and kakarikis. The prime site of attack is the bill, just below the cere (the soft section round the nostrils). The initial small tracks on the surface of the bill advance to form a coral-like encrustation that causes gross distortion of the bill.

Speed is important at the first sign of attack, because damage caused to the bill can be permanent. It seems probable that mites can be transferred when infected birds rub their bills against the perch to relieve itching, so isolation is advised.

One form of treatment is to rub the affected area with petroleum jelly (Vaseline), which interferes with the mite's respiration, but it can take several weeks for the condition to clear. Alternatively, there are proprietary preparations available.

Fleas, ticks and feather-lice

Fleas, ticks and feather-lice are encountered occasionally but can easily be eradicated with one of the many insecticidal sprays available for the purpose.

FEATHER-PLUCKING

This most familiar of all feather maladies is grossly disfiguring. Feather-plucking is a behavioural manifestation of a psychological condition triggered by stress. Most often encountered in the larger parrots, particularly those kept indoors, it is closely associated with boredom, but may also be a reflection of inadequate diet, the lack of breeding partner and the absence of bathing facilities – or a combination of all those factors.

Once the habit of feather-plucking starts it is difficult to eliminate, and may often reappear later in life, even after the original cause has been rectified. The behaviour can also occur in other species, including finches and softbills. In these cases it is usually associated with over-crowding, but can also be a response to irritation by parasites. As a precaution, regularly spray your pet birds with water and provide them with a stimulating, varied environment.

Feather-plucking, as on this Grey Parrot (Psittacus erithacus), is often the result of boredom.

A Flat Fly (Craterina hirundinis), as found among the feathers of many wild birds.

A budgerigar with a cancerous growth on its vent.

The overgrown upper mandible on this Laughing Dove (Streptopelia senegalensis) may have been the result of an injury as a fledgling.

TUMOURS

With the notable exception of budgerigars, 30 per cent or more of which are affected, tumours are quite uncommon in birds. Budgerigar keepers should maintain constant vigilance for signs of growths.

Birds that are fed a fatty diet risk developing lipomas, benign growths associated with obesity. The condition is self-perpetuating in that it induces lethargy, leading to further weight gain. Strict dieting may help, but surgery often proves to be the only lasting solution.

Budgerigars may also suffer from cancerous tumours of the reproductive system, possibly due to inbreeding, but lipomas are thought to be associated with dietary problems. All tumours, gradually and inescapably, lead to death. Besides gradual weight loss and increasing weakness, there is often a change in the colour of the cere, turning brown in cocks and blue in hens. This reflects a gender change, caused by the tumour, and sometimes results in corresponding shifts in behaviour.

BROKEN BONES AND OTHER ACCIDENTS

When accidents occur, whether bones are broken or bleeding injuries are sustained, birds invariably suffer from shock. Veterinary inspection is advised, particularly if internal injuries are suspected. Open bleeding wounds should first be cleaned with a mild antiseptic and any damaged feathers removed from the area. The flow of blood must be stemmed by the application of light pressure on a cotton gauze pad held in place by a tight bandage.

Although rough handling may occasionally lead to injury in birds, most fractures are the result of accidents, when frightened birds collide with solid objects. Fractured skulls, although rare, are usually fatal. Fractures of the long bones, however, can often be mended with careful treatment. If you suspect a fracture, keep the bird as quiet as possible and confined in the dark after wrapping it in a cloth or bandage to immobilize the area. Early veterinary help to set the break will improve the bird's chance of returning to normal. Remember that once the bone has set the associated muscles need time to rebuild as well.

A problem more or less confined to toucans and hornbills is fracture of the bill. Here, too, professional help is necessary. The bill must be restored properly if the bird is to be able to feed normally again.

MEDICATION

ANTIBIOTICS

Antibiotics are effective in the treatment of bacterial diseases, but have little effect on viral infections. Nevertheless, many veterinarians prescribe broad-spectrum antibiotics as a first line of treatment in a number of bird ailments, due to the need to start medication promptly. It is important that antibiotics are used precisely in the manner and dosage prescribed.

For small birds it is often easier to add antibiotic powder to the drinking water, if the bird is drinking regularly. The fluid intake of larger birds may not be sufficient for an effective dose and an injection may be necessary. Antibiotic powders can be mixed in with softbill food where appropriate.

Where tablets are prescribed, you will need to restrain the bird and place the tablet in the back of its throat, taking care to avoid the respiratory tract opening. Hold the bill closed for a few moments afterwards to encourage the bird to swallow.

After an antibiotic course of treatment, a probiotic must be added to the bird's diet to assist in the re-establishment of beneficial gut bacteria.

PROBIOTICS

Stress in birds reduces the effectiveness of the normal gut flora, thus increasing the bird's susceptibility to infections. This lowered resistance can be counteracted with the use of probiotics, which supply additional beneficial digestive bacteria, effectively keeping harmful bacteria in control and allowing for the most effective absorption of food.

Probiotics are available in dried and liquid forms. The liquid form is quicker acting, but as it is essentially a live bacterium it has a short shelf life. Dry probiotics, on the other hand, have to rehydrate and so are less readily absorbed by the digestive system.

Probiotics are frequently also used in preparing birds for breeding and encouraging the rapid growth of newly hatched chicks.

KEEPING YOUR BIRD HAPPY

Cage and aviary birds are susceptible to boredom if they are not provided with adequate mental stimulation. This is particularly true of inquisitive, intelligent birds such as parrots, budgerigars and their relatives.

Apart from the stimulus of human interaction, the needs of these birds can be satisfied by appropriate toys, which can keep them occupied for hours. A wide variety is available from pet shops, although many people create their own, particularly for the larger, more destructive species. A simple block of wood, securely suspended from the cage roof with wire, is usually adequate, but parrots also enjoy chewing the bark off twigs and breaking up pieces of wood.

For less destructive species, careful planting and an encouragement to forage increases the level of activity and reduces boredom. Several feeding sites, alternated at intervals, are often sufficient.

In most cases, one or two bird toys are enough; do not clutter cages with a large assortment. And make sure the toys are durable, safe and easy to clean. All toys must be free of sharp edges, while hanging toys must be secured safely to prevent injury. Thin cotton and wool are unsuitable, as birds can get tangled up and injure themselves. Toys on the cage floor quickly become soiled by droppings and require frequent cleaning.

LEFT *A Yellow-and-Green Lorikeet* – Trichoglossus flavoviridis meyeri.
FAR LEFT *Easy-to-make toys keep boredom at bay.*

DISPOSAL OF DEAD BIRDS

When a bird dies of an unknown cause, it is prudent to have a postmortem examination performed by a veterinarian, to determine the cause of death. Get advice from the vet immediately, and only deep-freeze the body once you are sure this will not destroy any useful pathological evidence.

Because of the possibility of disease, take special care to prevent the causative agents from spreading. This means isolating the corpse and anything it was in contact with as well as taking special care to wash your hands and everything that has been in contact with the bird very thoroughly in strong disinfectant.

Normally, the bird's body will be disposed of by the vet. If not, either bury it deeply (40–50cm; 15–20in) or incinerate it.

If the dead bird belonged to an exotic species, its body may be useful for scientific purposes or for display in your local natural history museum; in this case, deep-freeze the body in a well-sealed, thick polythene bag until you are able to deliver it.

COMPENDIUM OF BIRDS

PREVIOUS PAGES *It is not always possible to note the average size of a species, as size may depend on sex. In this example, the peacock is very much larger than the peafowl.*

ABOVE *Eastern Rosella* (Platycerus eximius)
TOP *Black-winged Lovebirds*

Just like humans, some birds get along well with each other and others do not. Compatibility does not only depend on individual sizes, but on factors such as species and the size of the aviary. Even with the relatively few species regularly kept in aviaries it would be impossible to list all those that can safely be kept together. Before putting any birds together, consider first of all how they behave in the wild. Some are sociable (living in colonies), while others are parasitic (dependent on host species). Others may be the opposite and will not tolerate any neighbours, even killing and eating them as prey.

If you want your aviary birds to breed, make sure you keep a pair separately. That way you can ensure little direct disturbance. This practice particularly applies to birds of the same species, unless they are colonial nesters, as in this way territorial disputes can be avoided.

When breeding is unlikely, keep the sexes of birds of the same species apart, otherwise quarrels will erupt. Males or females of the same species, housed on their own, will tolerate one another.

For mixed collections, the general rule is to keep birds of similar size and temperament together without overcrowding the aviary. Always be ready to

intervene at the first sign of trouble, and closely monitor any new bird. There will be an established pecking-order and any newcomer will be bullied if it is naturally less dominant.

On the following pages, a compendium of the major bird families suitable for cages and aviaries has been compiled, focusing on criteria such as the size of the bird and whether it is noisy or quiet, or hardy or delicate.

Great Hornbill (Buceros bicornis)

Size averages for the birds are not given where male and females differ greatly (for example, in pheasants and peafowl); here only the male's dimensions are shown (*). The size of a bird species varies depending on its sex and species, hence the length quoted in the table is only a guide.

Where possible, the birds are grouped together in families, but space restricts the inclusion of species to only a few of those available to aviculture. To help decide which bird suits a particular situation, the bird's qualities have been tabulated along with an indication of its suitablilty for cage or aviary. Delicate species obviously need additional care and protection in the more extreme climates. And do remember to take your neighbours into account when selecting birds: noisy creatures are likely to be a problem, especially in the early mornings.

QUAILS

These birds are ground nesters, usually hiding their eggs among tall grasses or under a dense shrub. Some quails lay clutches of as many as 15 eggs that take anywhere from 16–23 days to hatch. The young are mobile soon after hatching.

Larger quail thrive on turkey- or pheasant-rearing food and pellets, as well as insects, ant eggs and a little canary seed. Some enjoy berries and even chopped fruit. Small species such as the Blue-breasted Quail should be offered chick crumbs plus the seed mixture 3 and a few insects and ant eggs. For recently hatched young of this species, grind the crumbs to a smaller size.

Crested Partridge

California Quail

COMMON NAME	SCIENTIFIC NAME	SIZE	NOISY	QUIET	DELICATE	HARDY	CAGE	AVIARY
JAPANESE QUAIL	*Coturnix japonica*	18cm (7in)		●		●		●
BLUE-BREASTED QUAIL	*Coturnix chinensis*	14cm (5.5in)		●		●		●
CRESTED PARTRIDGE	*Rollulus rouloul*	26cm (10.3in)		●	●			●
SCALED QUAIL	*Callipepla squamata*	26cm (10.3in)		●	●			●
CALIFORNIA QUAIL	*Callipepla californica*	25cm (10in)		●		●		●
BANDED QUAIL	*Philortyx fasciatus*	20cm (8in)		●	●			●
NORTHERN BOBWHITE	*Colinus virginianus*	23cm (9in)	●			●		●

BARBETS

Barbets require a diet of fresh, chopped fruit and insects sprinkled with a soft food.

Most will use a sturdy nest box or hollow tree trunk layered with woodchips and placed high in the aviary. Some, such as the Crested Barbet, prefer rotting logs in which they excavate their own nests. Egg clutches vary from two to five. Incubation time is from 21–25 days and fledging, three weeks later.

Fire-tufted Barbet

Orange-fronted Barbet

COMMON NAME	SCIENTIFIC NAME	SIZE	NOISY	QUIET	DELICATE	HARDY	CAGE	AVIARY
FIRE-TUFTED BARBET	*Psilopogon pyrolophus*	26cm (10.3in)		●	●			●
LINEATED BARBET	*Megalaima lineata*	29cm (11.5in)		●	●			●
FLAME-FRONTED BARBET	*Megalaima armillaris*	20cm (8in)	●		●			●
COPPERSMITH BARBET	*Megalaima haemacephala*	15cm (6in)	●		●			●
SOWERBY'S BARBET	*Stactolaema whytii sowerbyi*	22cm (8.7in)		●	●			●
CRESTED BARBET	*Trachyphonus vaillantii*	20cm (8in)		●	●			●

TOUCANS

Toucans require a spacious aviary with carefully placed perches, giving them ample room to fly and perch without colliding with the structure. They are normally arboreal, requiring deep natural tree cavities with peat or aged woodchips in the base for roosting and nesting. Egg clutch size is usually from two to four, incubation taking 16–20 days. A long fledging time of six to 10 weeks should be expected.

Fresh, finely chopped fruit sprinkled with universal soft food plus insects, mice (pinkies) and ant eggs should be offered.

ABOVE *Red-billed Toucan*
RIGHT *Black-mandibled Toucan*

COMMON NAME	SCIENTIFIC NAME	SIZE	NOISY	QUIET	DELICATE	HARDY	CAGE	AVIARY
SPOT-BILLED TOUCANET	*Selenidera maculirostris*	29cm (11.5in)	●	●				●
RED-BILLED TOUCAN	*Ramphastos tucanus*	45cm (18in)	●	●				●
BLACK-MANDIBLED TOUCAN	*Ramphastos ambiguus swainsonii*	55cm (21.8in)	●	●				●

LORIES AND LORIKEETS

This group requires deep nest boxes or hollow logs lined with aged woodchips or dry peat in which to roost and nest. One to three eggs are laid, taking 24–27 days to incubate. The fledging period is from 50–80 days.

These birds feed on nectar and a fruit-based lorikeet diet; some species enjoy figs and insects.

Violet-necked Lory *Ornate Lory* *Weber's Lorikeet* *Red Lory*

COMMON NAME	SCIENTIFIC NAME	SIZE	NOISY	QUIET	DELICATE	HARDY	CAGE	AVIARY
VIOLET-NECKED LORY	*Eos squamata*	27cm (10.7in)	●			●		●
RED LORY	*Eos bornea*	31cm (12.3in)	●			●		●
ORNATE LORIKEET	*Trichoglossus ornatus*	25cm (10in)	●		●			●
MITCHELL'S LORIKEET	*Trichoglossus haematodus mitchelli*	30cm (12in)	●		●			●
WEBER'S LORIKEET	*Trichoglossus haematodus weberi*	28cm (11in)	●		●			●
SWAINSON'S LORIKEET	*Trichoglossus haematodus moluccanus*	30cm (12in)	●		●			●
GREEN-NAPED LORIKEET	*Trichoglossus haematodus haematodus*	30cm (12in)	●		●			●
YELLOW-AND-GREEN LORIKEET	*Trichoglossus flavoviridis*	21cm (8.3in)	●		●			●
CHATTERING LORY	*Lorius garrulus*	30cm (12in)	●			●		●
PURPLE-NAPED LORY	*Lorius domicella*	28cm (11in)	●			●		●
BLACK-CAPPED LORY	*Lorius lory*	31cm (12.3in)	●		●			●

COCKATOOS

For roosting and nesting, cockatoos require a nest box or hollow log lined with aged wood-chips or dry peat. The egg clutch size is normally two to five and incubation takes 23–27 days. Fledging time varies from eight to 12 weeks depending on the species.

A good diet consists of seed mixture 7 plus pelleted parrot food and chopped root vegetables, fruit and coconut. Insect larvae and berries are taken by some species.

Pink Cockatoo

Sulphur-crested Cockatoo

COMMON NAME	SCIENTIFIC NAME	SIZE	NOISY	QUIET	DELICATE	HARDY	CAGE	AVIARY
PINK COCKATOO	*Cacatua leadbeateri*	35cm (14in)	●			●		●
YELLOW-CRESTED COCKATOO	*Cacatua sulphurea*	33cm (13in)	●		●		●	●
SULPHUR-CRESTED COCKATOO	*Cacatua galerita*	50cm (20in)	●			●	●	●

MACAWS, PARROTS AND PARAKEETS

These birds, which originate from tropical regions, vary considerably in size. Consequently, breeding data is quite varied. In general, larger species have smaller egg clutch sizes of around two to four eggs and longer fledging times extending to as much as 12–14 weeks. Smaller parrots, referred to as parakeets, can lay as many as nine eggs in captivity, with fledging times often much shorter. Incubation can be three to four weeks. Most parrots will accept a nest box or hollow log with peat or aged woodchips in the base but some prefer to chew pieces of wood to create their own nest base.

The larger parrots should be offered seed mixture 7, whereas seed mixture 6 is more suitable for the smaller parakeets. Parrot pellets are an alternative, but a supplement of seeds and nuts gives a more varied diet. Corn-on-the-cob is enjoyed and many of these birds also benefit from additions of fresh diced fruit, grapes, berries, vegetables and a few pine nuts. Others will take insects and ant pupae. In the wild, some species such as the Red-winged Parrot, Yellow-fronted Parakeet and some 'Psittacula' parakeets take nectar and could therefore benefit from this addition to their diet.

Red-fronted Macaw

Grey Parrot

Sun Parakeets

COMMON NAME	SCIENTIFIC NAME	SIZE	NOISY	QUIET	DELICATE	HARDY	CAGE	AVIARY
MACAWS, PARROTS AND PARAKEETS								
BLUE-AND-YELLOW MACAW	*Ara ararauna*	86cm (34in)	●			●		●
RED-FRONTED MACAW	*Ara rubrogenys*	57cm (22.6in)	●			●		●
ECLECTUS PARROT	*Eclectus roratus*	39cm (15.5in)	●			●		●
RED-WINGED PARROT	*Aprosmictus erythropterus*	31cm (12.3in)	●			●		●
EASTERN ROSELLA	*Platycercus eximius*	30cm (12in)	●			●		●
RED-RUMPED PARROT	*Psephotus haematonotus*	27cm (10.7in)		●		●		●
ALEXANDRINE PARAKEET	*Psittacula eupatria*	58cm (23in)	●			●		●
ROSE-RINGED PARAKEET	*Psittacula krameri*	40cm (15.9in)	●			●		●
PLUM-HEADED PARAKEET	*Psittacula cyanocephala*	35cm (14in)		●	●			●
SUN PARAKEET	*Aratinga solstitialis*	30cm (12in)	●			●		●
BLUE-HEADED PARROT	*Pionus menstruus*	26cm (10.3in)	●			●		●
GREY PARROT	*Psittacus erithacus*	34cm (13.5in)	●			●	●	●
SENEGAL PARROT	*Poicephalus senegalus*	23cm (9in)	●			●		●
MEYER'S PARROT	*Poicephalus meyeri*	23cm (9in)	●			●		●
YELLOW-FRONTED PARAKEET	*Cyanoramphus auriceps*	23cm (9in)	●			●		●
CANARY-WINGED PARAKEET	*Brotogeris versicolurus*	22cm (8.7in)	●			●		●
TURQUOISE PARROT	*Neophema pulchella*	20cm (8in)		●		●		●

COCKATIELS, LOVEBIRDS AND HANGING PARROTS

Cockatiels are easy to keep, breed in aviaries and, as pets, thrive in large cages. A simple cockatiel nest box with a little dry peat or sawdust in the base is sufficient. Three to seven eggs are usually laid, taking just under three weeks to hatch. The young fledge in around four weeks. A simple diet of seed mixture 6 plus chopped apple, carrot, green food and seeding grasses should keep these birds fit and healthy.

Lovebirds normally nest in tree cavities or crevices and readily accept nest boxes with woodchips in the base. The three to eight eggs take about three weeks to hatch; chicks fledge up to seven weeks later. A good diet for lovebirds is seed mixture 5, plus millet sprays and occasionally chopped fruit, green food and paddy rice.

Hanging parrots normally frequent tree tops in tropical forests, nesting in tree cavities. In captivity a hole-type nest box lined with woodchips is sufficient. The two to four eggs take around three weeks to hatch and the chicks five weeks to fledge. Being nectivores, their recommended diet is spongecake soaked in nectar sprinkled with universal soft food plus diced fruit, berries and a few mealworms and insects. Some species benefit from small amounts of seed mixture 5.

Fischer's Lovebird

Cockatiels

Vernal Hanging Parrot

COMMON NAME	SCIENTIFIC NAME	SIZE	NOISY	QUIET	DELICATE	HARDY	CAGE	AVIARY
COCKATIELS, LOVEBIRDS AND HANGING PARROTS								
COCKATIEL	*Nymphicus hollandicus*	32cm (12.7in)	●			●	●	●
GREY-HEADED LOVEBIRD	*Agapornis canus*	15cm (6in)	●			●		●
BLACK-WINGED LOVEBIRD	*Agapornis taranta*	16cm (6.3in)	●			●		●
FISCHER'S LOVEBIRD	*Agapornis fischeri*	15cm (6in)	●			●		●
VERNAL HANGING PARROT	*Loriculus vernalis*	13cm (5in)		●		●		●
YELLOW-THROATED HANGING PARROT	*Loriculus pusillus*	12cm (4.7in)		●		●		●

HUMMINGBIRDS

These little birds seldom lay more than two eggs and incubation takes 13–15 days; fledging takes another 20–22 days. The nest is a tiny cup of hair, very fine plant fibres and spider-webs.

Nectar mixes make feeding relatively simple but scrupulous hygiene is essential for feeding utensils. Hummingbirds are attracted particularly to special feeding tubes with red spouts. To satisfy their need for small insects such as *Drosophila* and other fruit flies, a small breeding culture is very useful.

Wire-crested Thorntail Hummingbird

Booted Racquet-tail

COMMON NAME	SCIENTIFIC NAME	SIZE	NOISY	QUIET	DELICATE	HARDY	CAGE	AVIARY
RUBY-TOPAZ HUMMINGBIRD	*Chrysolampis mosquitus*	10cm (4in)		●	●			●
WIRE-CRESTED THORNTAIL	*Popelairia popelairii*	*13cm (5in)		●	●			●
BOOTED RACQUET-TAIL	*Discosura popelairii*	*13cm (5in)		●	●			●

TURACOS

Chopped fruit and vegetables, berries, fruit-based soft food, green food and mynah pellets are a suitable diet.

Provide a wicker or wire-mesh platform with twigs and plant fibres for nesting. Usually two eggs are laid and incubation takes 16–23 days. It can be up to four weeks before the young fledge.

White-cheeked Turaco

Hartlaub's Turaco

COMMON NAME	SCIENTIFIC NAME	SIZE	NOISY	QUIET	DELICATE	HARDY	CAGE	AVIARY
WHITE-CHEEKED TURACO	*Tauraco leucotis*	43cm (17in)	●			●		●
HARTLAUB'S TURACO	*Tauraco hartlaubi*	43cm (17in)	●			●		●

OWLS

Owls feed primarily on live food ranging from mammals, birds and reptiles to insects. In captivity, specially bred rats, mice (pinkies) and day-old chicks are adequate for the larger species, and insects and young rodents for the smaller. Finely diced fresh meat should also be offered.

Provide a nest box or hollow tree trunk for roosting and nesting. This should be set on the ground or into a bank for ground nesters like the Burrowing Owl. In captivity, clutch sizes can be up to seven eggs, taking anywhere from three to four weeks to hatch. Some species fledge in three weeks; others, like the Barn Owl, take up to seven.

Collared Scops Owl

Burrowing Owl

COMMON NAME	SCIENTIFIC NAME	SIZE	NOISY	QUIET	DELICATE	HARDY	CAGE	AVIARY
BARN OWL	*Tyto alba*	35cm (14in)	●			●		●
COMMON SCOPS OWL	*Otus scops*	20cm (8in)	●			●		●
COLLARED SCOPS OWL	*Otus bakkamoena*	20cm (8in)	●			●		●
TAWNY OWL	*Strix aluco*	22cm (8.7in)	●			●		●
BURROWING OWL	*Speyotyto cunicularia*	22cm (8.7in)	●			●		●

SEED-EATING DOVES

The seed-eating doves are relatively easy to feed, requiring little more than seed mixture 3 plus green food. Some species like the Namaqua Dove and Croaking Ground Dove are more insectivorous, requiring universal soft food and a few small insects.

Most species will accept a shelf, twig platform or wicker basket on which to construct a nest for which fine twigs and rootlets should be provided. Invariably, two eggs are laid that take around two weeks to hatch; chicks take two weeks to fledge.

RIGHT *Laughing Dove*
FAR RIGHT *Zebra Dove*

COMMON NAME	SCIENTIFIC NAME	SIZE	NOISY	QUIET	DELICATE	HARDY	CAGE	AVIARY
LAUGHING DOVE	*Streptopelia senegalensis*	27cm (10.7in)		●		●		●
SPOTTED DOVE	*Streptopelia chinensis*	29cm (11.5in)		●		●		●
BARBARY DOVE	*Streptopelia roseogrisea*	26cm (10.3in)		●		●		●
NAMAQUA DOVE	*Oena capensis*	28cm (11in)		●	●			●
DIAMOND DOVE	*Geopelia cuneata*	22cm (8.7in)		●		●		●
ZEBRA DOVE	*Geopelia striata*	21cm (8.3in)		●		●		●
EARED DOVE	*Zenaida auriculata*	25cm (10in)		●	●			●
CROAKING GROUND DOVE	*Columbina cruziana*	15cm (6in)		●	●			●

FRUIT-EATING DOVES

Wild fruit-doves feed almost entirely on fruit, but the variety available is considerable. In the aviary, a basic diet of finely chopped fruit sprinkled with universal soft food plus softbill pellets should be supplemented occasionally with ripe berries and figs. For nest construction, provide a twig platform or wicker basket with fine twigs and rootlets. One or two eggs are laid, taking around two to three weeks to hatch. The young take another two weeks to fledge.

Grey-cheeked Green Pigeon

COMMON NAME	SCIENTIFIC NAME	SIZE	NOISY	QUIET	DELICATE	HARDY	CAGE	AVIARY
PINK-NECKED GREEN-PIGEON	*Treron vernans*	26cm (10.3in)		●	●			●
GREY-CHEEKED GREEN-PIGEON	*Treron griseicauda*	26cm (10.3in)		●	●			●
BEAUTIFUL FRUIT-DOVE	*Ptilinopus pulchellus*	17cm (6.7in)		●	●			●
BLACK-NAPED FRUIT-DOVE	*Ptilinopus melanospila*	25cm (10in)		●	●			●

PITTAS

Pittas are ground-dwelling birds preferring to forage beneath leafy shrubs.

Their nest, a large, dome-shaped construction of grass and rootlets, is built among the undergrowth over a shallow depression in the ground. Normally a clutch of two eggs is laid, which takes up to three weeks to hatch. It takes a further three weeks before the young are fledged. When nesting, pittas can become aggressive and should therefore

have their own aviary, if at all possible. In the wild, pittas are insectivorous and occasionally take small mammals, reptiles and young birds.

In captivity, a diet of insectile soft food supplemented with live insects, small mammals, mealworms plus small mice (pinkies) is required.

Banded Pitta

COMMON NAME	SCIENTIFIC NAME	SIZE	NOISY	QUIET	DELICATE	HARDY	CAGE	AVIARY
BANDED PITTA	*Pitta guajana*	20cm (8in)		●	●			●

LEAFBIRDS

Leafbirds require a diet of finely chopped fruit sprinkled with universal soft food plus softbill pellets, mealworms and occasional nectar. Some will also take ant eggs.

They construct woven cup-shaped nests of roots and plant fibres in a dense shrub, or may use wicker nest baskets. Two to four eggs are laid which are incubated for two weeks. Fledging time is also two weeks.

RIGHT *Blue-winged Leafbird*
FAR RIGHT *Asian Fairy Bluebird*

COMMON NAME	SCIENTIFIC NAME	SIZE	NOISY	QUIET	DELICATE	HARDY	CAGE	AVIARY
LEAFBIRDS								
ASIAN FAIRY BLUEBIRD	*Irena puella*	25cm (10in)	●			●		●
GREATER GREEN LEAFBIRD	*Chloropsis sonnerati*	22cm (8.7in)	●			●		●
BLUE-WINGED LEAFBIRD	*Chloropsis cochinchinensis*	17cm (6.7in)	●			●		●
GOLDEN-FRONTED LEAFBIRD	*Chloropsis aurifrons*	19cm (7.5in)	●			●		●
ORANGE-BELLIED LEAFBIRD	*Chloropsis hardwickei*	20cm (8in)	●			●		●

SHRIKES

Shrikes thrive on large amounts of live food, especially grasshoppers, crickets, mealworms and wax moth larvae. This diet should be supplemented with softbill pellets and insectile soft food.

They construct an open, cup-shaped nest of grass and rootlets in the fork of a leafy shrub. Between three and six eggs are laid and incubated for about two weeks. The young fledge after another two weeks.

If a thorny branch is provided for the shrikes within the aviary, these birds will often impale food items on the thorns, just as they do in the wild.

ABOVE *Long-tailed Shrike*
RIGHT *Bay-backed Shrike*

COMMON NAME	SCIENTIFIC NAME	SIZE	NOISY	QUIET	DELICATE	HARDY	CAGE	AVIARY
LONG-TAILED SHRIKE	*Lanius schach*	23cm (9in)	●	●				●
BAY-BACKED SHRIKE	*Lanius vittatus*	18cm (7in)	●	●				●

JAYS, MAGPIES, CROWS AND ORIOLES

This group requires a basic diet of mynah pellets, universal soft food and insects. Many of them benefit from chopped fruit. Jays are usually fond of acorns, sunflower seed and peanuts. The Eurasian Jay and the magpies should also be offered mice (pinkies) and fresh, diced raw meat once a week.

Apart from the Black-naped Oriole, which constructs a neatly woven cup-shaped nest of rootlets and plant fibres, jays, magpies and crows build untidy nests of twigs, grasses and plant fibres in a cavity or dense shrub. Secure wire platforms and open-fronted nest boxes should be provided. Up to six eggs are laid. Incubation time approaches three weeks and fledging varies from three to four weeks.

ABOVE *Black-billed Magpie*
ABOVE LEFT *Black-chested Jay*
CENTRE *Black-naped Oriole*

COMMON NAME	SCIENTIFIC NAME	SIZE	NOISY	QUIET	DELICATE	HARDY	CAGE	AVIARY
JAYS, MAGPIES, CROWS AND ORIOLES								
CRESTED JAY	*Platylophus galericulatus*	28cm (11in)		●	●			●
BLACK-CHESTED JAY	*Cyanocorax affinis*	36cm (14.3in)		●	●			●
EURASIAN JAY	*Garrulus glandarius glandarius*	30cm (12in)	●			●		●
BLUE MAGPIE	*Urocissa erythrorhyncha*	66cm (26in)	●			●		●
RACQUET-TAILED TREEPIE	*Crypsirina temia*	35cm (14in)		●	●			●
BLACK-BILLED MAGPIE	*Pica pica*	50cm (20in)	●			●		●
EURASIAN JACKDAW	*Corvus monedula*	33cm (13in)	●			●		●
BLACK-NAPED ORIOLE	*Oriolus chinensis*	26cm (10.3in)	●		●			●

MINIVETS AND WAXWINGS

A diet for minivets consists of finely chopped fruit sprinkled with insectivorous soft food and a plentiful supply of small insects. The same diet is satisfactory for waxwings but with the addition of berries.

Both families construct cup-shaped nests of grass stems, fine twigs, moss and plant fibres in the fork of a leafy shrub, but the larger waxwing nests benefit from a platform of twigs or wickerwork. Three to five eggs are laid, taking two weeks to incubate. The young take two weeks to fledge.

Scarlet Minivet   *Cedar Waxwing*

COMMON NAME	SCIENTIFIC NAME	SIZE	NOISY	QUIET	DELICATE	HARDY	CAGE	AVIARY
SCARLET MINIVET	*Pericrocotus flammeus*	19cm (7.5in)		●	●			●
CEDAR WAXWING	*Bombycilla cedrorum*	15cm (6in)		●		●		●

THRUSHES AND FLYCATCHERS

Apart from the Siberian Rubythroat, which requires a diet consisting of insectivorous soft food plus small insects and ant pupae, other birds in this group will accept a more fruit-based diet of finely chopped fruit sprinkled with universal soft food plus berries, mealworms, waxworms and crickets. Thrushes also enjoy occasional earthworms. Oriental Magpie Robins and White-rumped Shamas can benefit from additions of soaked mynah pellets.

This group constructs cup-shaped nests of fine twigs, grasses and plant fibres in dense shrubs. Some use moss and hair; others, like the Orange-headed Thrush and Eurasian Blackbird, incorporate mud. The clutch of three to six eggs takes two weeks to incubate. The young fledge around two weeks later.

ABOVE *Orange-headed Thrush*
LEFT *Verditer Flycatcher*

COMMON NAME	SCIENTIFIC NAME	SIZE	NOISY	QUIET	DELICATE	HARDY	CAGE	AVIARY
THRUSHES AND FLYCATCHERS								
ORANGE-HEADED THRUSH	*Zoothera citrina*	21cm (8.3in)		●	●			●
EURASIAN BLACKBIRD	*Turdus merula*	25cm (10in)		●		●		●
VERDITER FLYCATCHER	*Eumyias thalassina*	15cm (6in)		●	●			●
RUFOUS-BELLIED NILTAVA	*Niltava sundara*	15cm (6in)		●	●			●
HILL BLUE FLYCATCHER	*Cyornis banyumas*	15cm (6in)		●	●			●
SIBERIAN RUBYTHROAT	*Luscinia calliope*	14cm (5.5in)		●		●		●
ORIENTAL MAGPIE ROBIN	*Copsychus saularis*	20cm (8in)		●	●			●
WHITE-RUMPED SHAMA	*Copsychus malabaricus*	28cm (11in)		●	●			●

STARLINGS AND MYNAHS

Starlings and mynahs construct untidy nests of twigs, grass, plant fibres, rootlets and hair in a nest box or hollow log with a hole towards the top.

Apart from the Hill Mynah, which requires a hole of 7–8cm (3in) in diameter, and the small Asian Glossy Starling, which will pass through a 5cm (2in) hole, all the other starlings and mynahs are happy to accept nest boxes with holes of about 6cm (2.5in) in diameter.

Two to six eggs are to be expected, taking around two weeks to incubate. The young take up to three or four weeks to fledge.

The diet consists of mynah pellets plus chopped fruit sprinkled with universal soft food and insects. The Hill Mynah, a larger bird, will accept large insects and sometimes small mice (pinkies).

ABOVE *Common Mynah*
ABOVE LEFT *Golden-breasted Starling*
FOLLOWING PAGES *Greater Hill Mynah*

COMMON NAME	SCIENTIFIC NAME	SIZE	NOISY	QUIET	DELICATE	HARDY	CAGE	AVIARY
ASIAN GLOSSY STARLING	*Aplonis panayensis*	20cm (8in)		●	●			●
PURPLE GLOSSY STARLING	*Lamprotornis purpureus*	23cm (9in)		●	●			●
GREATER BLUE-EARED GLOSSY-STARLING	*Lamprotornis chalybaeus*	20cm (8in)		●	●			●
SUPERB STARLING	*Lamprotornis superbus*	20cm (8in)		●		●		●
GOLDEN-BREASTED STARLING	*Cosmopsarus regius*	35cm (14in)		●	●			●
CHESTNUT-TAILED STARLING	*Sturnus malabaricus*	20cm (8in)		●	●			●
BRAHMINY STARLING (MYNAH)	*Sturnus pagodarum*	20cm (8in)	●		●			●
PURPLE-BACKED STARLING	*Sturnus sturninus*	20cm (8in)		●		●		●
ROSY STARLING	*Sturnus roseus*	20cm (8in)		●		●		●
COMMON STARLING	*Sturnus vulgaris*	22cm (8.7in)		●		●		●
ASIAN PIED STARLING (MYNAH)	*Sturnus contra*	24cm (9.5in)		●		●		●
COMMON MYNAH	*Acridotheres tristis*	24cm (9.5in)	●			●		●
CRESTED MYNAH	*Acridotheres cristatellus*	26cm (10.3in)		●		●		●
HILL MYNAH	*Gracula religiosa*	30cm (12in)	●			●	●	●
FINCH-BILLED MYNAH	*Scissirostrum dubium*	21cm (8.3in)		●	●			●

NUTHATCHES

Contrary to what the name infers, this family is mainly insectivorous, depending on seeds and nuts in temperate regions only when harsher weather conditions destroy or limit the available insect population. Some northern species, therefore, consume a wide choice of food, while the tropical species are more insectivorous.

Species from temperate regions require seed mixture 3 plus green food, insectivorous soft food, small insects, ant pupae and peanuts. Tropical species should have a bias towards insectivorous foods with less seed.

Birds of this family construct cup-shaped nests of bark flakes and woodchips in tree hollows. In the aviary, a nest box with a 4cm (1.5in) diameter hole should be provided, along with wet mud for the customary plastering around the entrance hole.

Clutch sizes vary from three to four in the tropics, to six to eight in temperate regions. Incubation is a little over two weeks and rearing from three to four.

Velvet-fronted Nuthatch

COMMON NAME	SCIENTIFIC NAME	SIZE	NOISY	QUIET	DELICATE	HARDY	CAGE	AVIARY
EURASIAN NUTHATCH	*Sitta europaea*	14cm (5.5in)		●		●		●
VELVET-FRONTED NUTHATCH	*Sitta frontalis*	14cm (5.5in)		●	●			●

BULBULS

Bulbuls construct cup-shaped nests of grass stems, moss and plant fibres in shrubs or secluded open-fronted nest boxes. Between two and five eggs are laid, which take two weeks to incubate. Fledging usually takes just under two weeks.

These softbills require a diet of finely chopped fruit sprinkled with universal soft food plus softbill pellets, mealworms and occasional nectar.

While nesting, bulbuls can be very territorial indeed, causing great distress to the other birds that may be occupying the same aviary. It is therefore better, wherever possible, to keep them separate at this time.

Red-vented Bulbul

Sooty-headed Bulbul

COMMON NAME	SCIENTIFIC NAME	SIZE	NOISY	QUIET	DELICATE	HARDY	CAGE	AVIARY
BLACK-HEADED BULBUL	*Pycnonotus atriceps*	17cm (6.7in)		●	●			●
LIGHT-VENTED BULBUL	*Pycnonotus sinensis*	23cm (9in)		●		●		●
RED-VENTED BULBUL	*Pycnonotus cafer*	20cm (8in)	●		●			●
SOOTY-HEADED BULBUL	*Pycnonotus aurigaster*	20cm (8in)		●		●		●
ORANGE-SPOTTED BULBUL	*Pycnonotus bimaculatus*	20cm (8in)		●	●			●
YELLOW-VENTED BULBUL	*Pycnonotus goiavier*	20cm (8in)		●	●			●
GREY-CHEEKED BULBUL	*Alophoixus bres*	22cm (8.3in)		●	●			●

WHITE-EYES

A suitable diet for white-eyes consists of finely chopped fruit and green food sprinkled with universal soft food plus nectar, crushed softbill pellets and small insects.

The cup-shaped nest is made of moss, hair, plant fibres and spider-webs, in dense vegetation. Up to four eggs are laid, with incubation taking 12 days. Fledging time is two weeks.

Chestnut-flanked White-eye

Mountain White-eye

COMMON NAME	SCIENTIFIC NAME	SIZE	NOISY	QUIET	DELICATE	HARDY	CAGE	AVIARY
AFRICAN YELLOW WHITE-EYE	*Zosterops senegalensis*	10cm (4in)		●	●			●
CHESTNUT-FLANKED WHITE-EYE	*Zosterops erythropleurus*	12cm (4.7in)		●	●			●
ORIENTAL WHITE-EYE	*Zosterops palpebrosus*	11cm (4.4in)		●	●			●
MOUNTAIN WHITE-EYE	*Zosterops montanus*	11cm (4.4in)		●	●			●

LAUGHINGTHRUSHES AND BABBLERS

Laughingthrushes and other large babblers require a diet of finely chopped fruit sprinkled with insectivorous soft food plus a few mynah pellets, mealworms, wax moth larvae, crickets and ant pupae when available. The Yuhinas are partly nectivorous, so in addition to insectivorous soft food, finely chopped fruit and fruit-fly larvae, they should also be offered spongecake soaked in nectar.

This group of birds constructs cup-shaped nests of grass, rootlets and plant fibres in dense shrubs. In the wild, the Silver-eared Mesia uses dry bamboo leaves rather than grass for the basic construction, so offering this material in the aviary could improve chances of breeding. Similarly, Rufous Sibias should be offered pine needles, hair and feathers in addition to rootlets and plant fibres, while Yuhinas require moss, hair, plant fibres and spider-webs. The Red-billed Leiothrix (Pekin Robin) favours crevices, so an open-fronted nest box is appropriate. A clutch of three to four eggs is incubated for about two weeks and fledging usually occurs about two weeks later.

ABOVE *Rusty-cheeked Scimitar-Babbler*
ABOVE RIGHT *Yellow-throated Laughingthrush*
RIGHT *Chinese Babax*
BELOW *Rufous Sibia*

LAUGHINGTHRUSHES AND BABBLERS

COMMON NAME	SCIENTIFIC NAME	SIZE	NOISY	QUIET	DELICATE	HARDY	CAGE	AVIARY
WHITE-THROATED LAUGHINGTHRUSH	*Garrulax albogularis*	28cm (11in)	•			•		•
WHITE-CRESTED LAUGHINGTHRUSH	*Garrulax leucolophus*	29cm (11.5in)	•			•		•
BLACK-THROATED LAUGHINGTHRUSH	*Garrulax chinensis*	23cm (9in)	•			•		•
YELLOW-THROATED LAUGHINGTHRUSH	*Garrulax galbanus*	23cm (9in)	•		•			•
RUSTY LAUGHINGTHRUSH	*Garrulax poecilorhynchus*	28cm (11in)	•		•			•
RUSTY-CHEEKED SCIMITAR-BABBLER	*Pomatorhinus erythrogenys*	29cm (11.5in)		•		•		•
CHESTNUT-BACKED SCIMITAR-BABBLER	*Pomatorhinus montanus*	20cm (8in)		•	•			•
CHINESE BABAX	*Babax lanceolatus*	26cm (10.3in)		•	•			•
SILVER-EARED MESIA	*Leiothrix argentauris*	18cm (7in)		•		•		•
RED-BILLED LEIOTHRIX	*Leiothrix lutea*	15cm (6in)		•		•		•
RUFOUS SIBIA	*Heterophasia capistrata*	25cm (10in)		•	•			•
WHISKERED YUHINA	*Yuhina flavicollis*	10cm (4in)		•	•			•
BLACK-CHINNED YUHINA	*Yuhina nigrimenta*	10cm (4in)		•	•			•

PARROTBILLS

Parrotbills require a diet consisting of seed mixture 3 plus green food, finely chopped fruit, insectivorous soft food, small insects and ant pupae. Some mealworms and occasional offerings of soaked and sprouted seed are relished. Parrotbills construct cup-shaped nests of grasses, lining them with moss, hair and plant fibres. A clutch of three or four eggs is laid, with incubation taking around 12 days and fledging about the same time.

RIGHT *Grey-headed Parrotbill*

COMMON NAME	SCIENTIFIC NAME	SIZE	NOISY	QUIET	DELICATE	HARDY	CAGE	AVIARY
GREY-HEADED PARROTBILL	*Paradoxornis gularis*	17cm (6.7in)		•		•		•

SUNBIRDS

Sunbirds require nectar and small insects plus finely chopped soft fruit.

This family of birds constructs delicately suspended, purse-shaped nests from fine grasses, plant fibres, hairs and spider-webs. Two eggs are laid, taking two weeks to incubate. The young take two weeks to fledge.

RIGHT *Purple-banded Sunbird*

COMMON NAME	SCIENTIFIC NAME	SIZE	NOISY	QUIET	DELICATE	HARDY	CAGE	AVIARY
PURPLE-THROATED SUNBIRD	*Nectarinia sperata sperata*	10cm (4in)		•	•			•
PURPLE-BANDED SUNBIRD	*Nectarinia bifasciata*	13cm (5in)		•	•			•
FORK-TAILED SUNBIRD	*Aethopyga christinae latouchi*	16cm (6.3in)		•	•			•

SPARROWS, WEAVERS AND WIDOWBIRDS

These small seed-eaters flourish on seed mixture S3 plus green food and seeding grasses, paddy rice, millet sprays and a few insects.

The Sudan Golden Sparrow normally constructs a globular nest of thorny twigs lined with grasses, bark, leaves and feathers in a shrub, but will use a nest box with a 6cm (2.3in) diameter hole. In general, weavers use grasses and plant fibres to weave nests of different shapes and sizes suspended in a shrub or among vertical branches or reeds. Several species will use open-fronted nest boxes and wicker baskets, which should be hidden among thick foliage.

Vitelline-masked Weaver

Most lay clutches of two to four eggs, but there may be six. Incubation time is about two weeks, with fledging taking two to three.

Sudan Golden Sparrow

Yellow-mantled Widowbird

COMMON NAME	SCIENTIFIC NAME	SIZE	NOISY	QUIET	DELICATE	HARDY	CAGE	AVIARY
SUDAN GOLDEN SPARROW	*Passer luteus*	13cm (5in)	●	●				●
GOLDEN PALM WEAVER	*Ploceus bojeri*	15cm (6in)	●	●				●
RUEPPELL'S WEAVER	*Ploceus galbula*	15cm (6in)	●	●				●
VITELLINE-MASKED WEAVER	*Ploceus vitellinus*	13cm (5in)	●			●		●
BAYA WEAVER	*Ploceus philippinus*	15cm (6in)	●	●				●
RED-HEADED QUELEA	*Quelea erythrops*	13cm (5in)	●			●		●
RED-BILLED QUELEA	*Quelea quelea*	13cm (5in)	●			●		●
MADAGASCAR RED FODY	*Foudia madagascariensis*	13cm (5in)	●			●		●
YELLOW-CROWNED BISHOP	*Euplectes afer*	13cm (5in)	●			●		●
RED BISHOP	*Euplectes orix*	14cm (5.5in)	●			●		●
FAN-TAILED WIDOWBIRD	*Euplectes axillaris*	18cm (7in)	●	●				●
YELLOW-MANTLED WIDOWBIRD	*Euplectes macrourus macrourus*	22cm (8.7in)	●	●				●
RED-COLLARED WIDOWBIRD	*Euplectes ardens*	15cm (6in)	●	●				●

PYTILIAS, TWINSPOTS AND FIREFINCHES

Mainly seed-eaters, this group requires a simple diet of seed mixture 3 plus spray millet, green food and a few small insects.

They build nests of plant fibres and fine grasses lined with hair and feathers, low down in a shrub. Two to four eggs are laid, taking 12–13 days to incubate. The young take about three weeks to fledge.

Green-winged Pytilia

Peter's Twinspot

COMMON NAME	SCIENTIFIC NAME	SIZE	NOISY	QUIET	DELICATE	HARDY	CAGE	AVIARY
RED-WINGED PYTILIA	*Pytilia phoenicoptera*	13cm (5in)		●		●		●
GREEN-WINGED PYTILIA	*Pytilia melba*	13cm (5in)		●		●		●
GREEN-BACKED TWINSPOT	*Mandingoa nitidula*	10cm (4in)		●		●		●
SCHLEGEL'S TWINSPOT	*Mandingoa nitidula schlegeli*	10cm (4in)		●		●		●
PETER'S TWINSPOT	*Hypargos niveoguttatus*	13cm (5in)		●		●		●
RED-BILLED FIREFINCH	*Lagonosticta senegala*	9cm (3.5in)		●		●		●

WAXBILLS

In the wild many waxbills take insects, so this should be reflected in the diet offered. Seed mixture 3 plus green food, universal soft food, millet sprays and small insects should be given.

Their nests are woven, dome-shaped or globular structures constructed of fine grass and feathers in a secluded shrub or open-fronted nest box. Up to eight eggs take around two weeks to incubate with the young fledging about three weeks later.

Common Waxbill

Green Avadavat

COMMON NAME	SCIENTIFIC NAME	SIZE	NOISY	QUIET	DELICATE	HARDY	CAGE	AVIARY
RED-CHEEKED CORDONBLEU	*Uraeginthus bengalus*	12cm (4.7in)		●	●			●
BLUE-CAPPED CORDONBLEU	*Uraeginthus cyanocephala*	13cm (5in)		●	●			●
PURPLE GRENADIER	*Uraeginthus ianthinogaster*	13cm (5in)		●	●			●
ORANGE-CHEEKED WAXBILL	*Estrilda melpoda*	10cm (4in)		●	●			●
BLACK-RUMPED WAXBILL	*Estrilda troglodytes*	10cm (4in)		●	●			●
COMMON WAXBILL	*Estrilda astrild*	11cm (4.4in)		●		●		●
BLACK-CHEEKED WAXBILL	*Estrilda erythronotos*	10cm (4in)		●	●			●
RED AVADAVAT	*Amandava amandava*	10cm (4in)		●		●		●
GREEN AVADAVAT	*Amandava formosa*	10cm (4in)		●	●			●
ZEBRA WAXBILL	*Amandava subflava*	9cm (3.5in)		●	●			●

PARASITIC WHYDAHS

These birds are dependent on the correct host to improve their chances of successful breeding. In the aviary environment this may mean that a successful breeding colony of the host species must be established first.

The Village Indigobird is partially parasitic on the Red-billed Fire-finch (*Lagonosticta rufopicta*), but is known to construct its own nest of grasses and plant fibres occasionally. It may use an open-fronted nest box, wicker basket or old weaver's nest. Three or four eggs are laid that take 12 days to incubate and two weeks for the young to fledge.

The Straw-tailed Whydah's host is the Purple Grenadier Waxbill (*Uraeginthus ianthinogaster*) and the Pin-tailed Whydah will use St Helena (*Estrilda astrild*), Red-eared (*Estrilda troglodytes*) and Orange-cheeked (*Estrilda melpoda*) Waxbills.

All whydahs are seed-eaters, requiring a diet of seed mixture 3 plus green food, paddy rice, seeding grasses and millet sprays.

ABOVE *(Straw-tailed) Fischer's Whydah*
LEFT *Pin-tailed Whydah*

COMMON NAME	SCIENTIFIC NAME	SIZE	NOISY	QUIET	DELICATE	HARDY	CAGE	AVIARY
VILLAGE INDIGOBIRD	*Vidua chalybeata*	13cm (5in)		●	●			●
STRAW-TAILED WHYDAH	*Vidua fischeri*	*30cm (12in)		●	●			●
PIN-TAILED WHYDAH	*Vidua macroura*	*30cm (12in)		●		●		●

SMALL FINCHES

Small finches thrive on seed mixture 3 plus green food, a little universal soft food, millet sprays and a few small insects.

They build cup-shaped nests, sometimes domed, in shrubs, but many will also use an open-fronted nest box. Fine grasses, plant fibres, rootlets, feathers and hairs should all be provided. Four to six eggs are normal, with incubation taking 12–14 days and fledging about three weeks.

RIGHT *Cut-throat Weaver*
CENTRE *Zebra Finch*
FAR RIGHT *Pin-tailed Parrotfinch*

COMMON NAME	SCIENTIFIC NAME	SIZE	NOISY	QUIET	DELICATE	HARDY	CAGE	AVIARY
SMALL FINCHES								
DIAMOND FIRETAIL	*Staganopleura guttata*	13cm (5in)		●		●		●
STAR FINCH	*Neochmia ruficauda*	11cm (4.4in)		●		●		●
PLUM-HEADED FINCH	*Neochmia modesta*	11cm (4.4in)		●		●		●
ZEBRA FINCH	*Taeniopygia guttata*	10cm (4in)		●		●	●	●
DOUBLE-BARRED FINCH	*Taeniopygia bichenovii*	11cm (4.4in)		●		●		●
LONG-TAILED FINCH	*Poephila acuticauda*	16cm (6.3in)		●		●	●	●
PIN-TAILED PARROTFINCH	*Erythrura prasina*	14cm (5.5in)		●		●		●
GOULDIAN FINCH	*Chloebia gouldiae*	14cm (5.5in)		●		●		●
JAVA SPARROW	*Padda oryzivora*	14cm (5.5in)		●		●	●	●
CUT-THROAT WEAVER	*Amadina fasciata*	13cm (5in)		●		●		●
RED-HEADED FINCH	*Amadina erythrocephala*	13cm (5in)		●		●		●

MUNIAS

In the wild, many of the munias are renowned for gathering in large flocks to raid cultivated rice crops. Although they are generally considered seed-eaters, some of this group are more omnivorous. A basic diet of seed mixture 3 plus green food, paddy rice, seeding grasses and millet sprays is required plus a little universal soft food and a few small insects.

Many weave nests of fine grasses, plant fibres, rootlets and feathers, either in a shrub or suspended among thin bamboos, reeds or grasses. Others will use a nest basket or an open-fronted nest box. The usual clutch size is four to six, but the Bengalese Finch will often lay up to eight. Incubation takes 12–14 days and fledging three weeks.

Scaly-breasted Munia

Chestnut Munia

COMMON NAME	SCIENTIFIC NAME	SIZE	NOISY	QUIET	DELICATE	HARDY	CAGE	AVIARY
MADAGASCAR MUNIA	*Lemuresthes nana*	10cm (4in)		●		●		●
WHITE-THROATED SILVERBILL	*Lonchura malabarica*	10cm (4in)		●		●		●
BRONZE MUNIA	*Lonchura cucullata*	10cm (4in)		●		●		●
MAGPIE MUNIA	*Lonchura fringilloides*	13cm (5in)		●		●		●
BENGALESE FINCH	*Lonchura domestica*	13cm (5in)		●		●	●	●
SCALY-BREASTED MUNIA	*Lonchura punctulata*	12cm (4.7in)		●		●		●
BLACK-HEADED MUNIA	*Lonchura malacca*	12cm (4.7in)		●		●		●
SOUTHERN BLACK-HEADED MUNIA	*Lonchura malacca atricapilla*	12cm (4.7in)		●		●		●
WHITE-HEADED MUNIA	*Lonchura maja*	12cm (4.7in)		●		●		●
CHESTNUT-BREASTED MUNIA	*Lonchura castaneothorax*	13cm (5in)		●		●		●
BLACK MUNIA	*Lonchura stygia*	12cm (4.7in)		●		●		●

FINCHES

Most finches are primarily seed-eaters requiring a basic diet of seed mixture 3 plus green food, but many will benefit from a little insectivorous soft food and a few insects.

They construct cup-shaped nests of plant fibres, grasses, twigs, rootlets and moss, often lined with hair and feathers and positioned in a dense shrub. Some will use an open-fronted nest box. The egg clutch size is usually four but some species lay up to six. Incubation time is around two weeks with another two weeks for the young to fledge.

Eurasian Bullfinch

Black-headed Greenfinch

European Goldfinch

COMMON NAME	SCIENTIFIC NAME	SIZE	NOISY	QUIET	DELICATE	HARDY	CAGE	AVIARY
WHITE-RUMPED SEED-EATER	Serinus leucopygius	13cm (5in)		●		●		●
YELLOW-RUMPED SEED-EATER	Serinus atrogularis	14cm (5.5in)		●		●		●
YELLOW-FRONTED CANARY	Serinus mozambicus	13cm (5in)		●		●		●
STREAKY-HEADED SEED-EATER	Serinus gularis	14cm (5.5in)		●		●		●
EUROPEAN GREENFINCH	Carduelis chloris	16cm (6.3in)		●		●		●
BLACK-HEADED GREENFINCH	Carduelis spinoides	13cm (5in)		●		●		●
EURASIAN SISKIN	Carduelis spinus	12cm (4.7in)		●		●		●
RED SISKIN	Carduelis cucullata	10cm (4in)		●	●			●
EUROPEAN GOLDFINCH	Carduelis carduelis	14cm (5.5in)		●		●		●
COMMON REDPOLL	Carduelis flammea	15cm (6in)		●		●		●
EURASIAN LINNET	Carduelis cannabina	14cm (5.5in)		●		●		●
HOUSE FINCH	Carpodacus mexicanus	15cm (6in)		●		●		●
EURASIAN BULLFINCH	Pyrrhula pyrrhula	15cm (6in)		●		●		●
BEAVAN'S BULLFINCH	Pyrrhula erythaca	15cm (6in)		●		●		●

LARGE FINCHES

This group has slightly different feeding habits to the smaller finches and requires a diet consisting of seed mixture 4 plus green food, berries, chopped fruit and small pine nuts. Like other, smaller finches, they will benefit from a little insectivorous food and a few insects.

They construct cup-shaped nests of long thick twigs, rootlets and grasses, lined with rootlets and hair, in a shrub. Three to six eggs are laid, taking two weeks to incubate. The young take another two weeks to fledge.

RIGHT *White-rumped Seed-eater*

COMMON NAME	SCIENTIFIC NAME	SIZE	NOISY	QUIET	DELICATE	HARDY	CAGE	AVIARY
HAWFINCH	Coccothraustes coccothraustes	18cm (7in)		●		●		●
JAPANESE GROSBEAK	Euphona personata	19cm (7.5in)		●		●		●

BUNTINGS AND CARDINALS

The smaller birds in this group require a diet consisting of seed mixture 3 plus a little chopped fruit and green food, insectivorous soft food and live insects. The larger birds, such as the cardinals, require some larger seed as well as berries, so it is appropriate to give seed mixture 4 in place of 3.

These birds build cup-shaped nests of grasses and rootlets or moss, lined with hair and feathers in wicker nesting baskets secluded in dense shrubs or among climbing plants. Egg clutch sizes vary from two to three – and sometimes up to five. Incubation takes about two weeks, followed by two weeks to fledging.

ABOVE *Red-cowled Cardinal*
LEFT *African Golden-breasted Bunting*

COMMON NAME	SCIENTIFIC NAME	SIZE	NOISY	QUIET	DELICATE	HARDY	CAGE	AVIARY
AFRICAN GOLDEN-BREASTED BUNTING	*Emberiza flaviventris*	17cm (6.7in)		●	●			●
RED-HEADED BUNTING	*Emberiza bruniceps*	16cm (6.3in)		●		●		●
RUFOUS-COLLARED SPARROW	*Zonotrichia capensis*	15cm (6in)		●		●		●
YELLOW CARDINAL	*Gubernatrix cristata*	19cm (7.5in)		●	●			●
RED-COWLED CARDINAL	*Paroaria dominicana*	18cm (7in)		●	●			●
NORTHERN CARDINAL	*Cardinalis cardinalis*	23cm (9in)		●		●		●

TANAGERS

In the wild, tanagers feed on fruit, berries and seeds, often supplemented with nectar and insects. To replicate this in captivity, chopped fruit and green food sprinkled with universal soft food and seed mixture 3, supplemented regularly with nectar and live insects, is advised.

Most will build a deep, cup-shaped nest of rootlets, green moss, dead leaves, grasses and plant fibres in a dense shrub, and others will use a wicker basket or open-fronted nest box. Some of the smaller species also incorporate spider-webs. Normally two eggs are laid, taking between 12–16 days to incubate. Fledging time varies from 12–28 days, depending on the species.

Seven-coloured Tanager

Opal-rumped Tanager

COMMON NAME	SCIENTIFIC NAME	SIZE	NOISY	QUIET	DELICATE	HARDY	CAGE	AVIARY
SILVER-BEAKED TANAGER	*Ramphocelus carbo*	17cm (6.7in)	●	●		●		●
BLUE-GREY TANAGER	*Thraupis episcopus*	16cm (6.3in)	●	●		●		●
BLUE-CAPPED TANAGER	*Thraupis cyanocephala*	16cm (6.3in)	●	●		●		●
BLUE-WINGED MOUNTAIN TANAGER	*Anisognathus flavinuchus flavinuchus*	17cm (6.7in)	●	●		●		●
YELLOW-CROWNED EUPHONIA	*Euphonia luteicapilla*	9cm (3.5in)	●	●		●		●
YELLOW-BELLIED TANAGER	*Tangara xanthrogastra*	11cm (4.4in)	●	●		●		●
SPOTTED TANAGER	*Tangara punctata*	12cm (4.7in)	●	●		●		●
GOLDEN-HOODED TANAGER	*Tangara larvata*	12cm (4.7in)	●	●		●		●
SEVEN-COLOURED TANAGER	*Tangara fastuosa*	13cm (5in)	●	●		●		●
GREEN & GOLD TANAGER	*Tangara schrankii*	12cm (4.7in)	●	●		●		●
GOLDEN TANAGER	*Tangara arthus aurulenta*	13cm (5in)	●	●		●		●
SILVER-THROATED TANAGER	*Tangara icterocephala*	13cm (5in)	●	●		●		●
BLUE-NECKED TANAGER	*Tangara cyanicollis*	12cm (4.7in)	●	●		●		●
OPAL RUMPED TANAGER	*Tangara velia*	14cm (5.5in)	●	●		●		●

BANANAQUITS AND HONEYCREEPERS

In addition to nectar, chopped fruit and green food sprinkled with universal soft food, small ripe berries and small fruit flies should be given. This group of birds also consumes varying amounts of small seeds in the wild, so a little seed mixture 3 could be beneficial. The young are normally fed on small live insects and spiders.

The Bananaquit builds a globular-shaped nest of rootlets, moss and grasses low in a dense shrub, whereas honeycreepers have cup-shaped nests of fine plant fibres, moss, spider-webs and leaves suspended in a fork of a shrub. The clutch of two or three eggs is incubated for about 13 days and the young fledge in just over two weeks.

RIGHT *Bananaquit*
FAR RIGHT *Golden-collared Honeycreeper*

COMMON NAME	SCIENTIFIC NAME	SIZE	NOISY	QUIET	DELICATE	HARDY	CAGE	AVIARY
BANANAQUIT	*Coereba flaveola*	12cm (4.7in)	●	●				●
GOLDEN-COLLARED HONEYCREEPER	*Tangara pulcherrima*	11cm (4.4in)	●	●				●
PURPLE HONEYCREEPER	*Cyanerpes caeruleus*	10cm (4in)	●	●				●
RED-LEGGED HONEYCREEPER	*Cyanerpes cyaneus*	12cm (4.7in)	●	●				●

NEW WORLD FINCHES

The smaller of these finches require a diet consisting of seed mixture S3 plus green food, a little chopped fruit and a few mealworms and crickets. The Red-crested Finch should be given seed mixture 4 in place of seed mixture 3, while the stronger-billed *Sporophila* species needs the larger seeds as provided in mixture 6.

Finches build cup-shaped nests of grasses, twigs and moss, lined with hair and feathers, well-hidden in a dense shrub. Some will accept an open-fronted nest box. Two to four eggs are laid. Incubation takes around two weeks and fledging another two weeks.

Red-crested Finch

White-collared Seed-eater

COMMON NAME	SCIENTIFIC NAME	SIZE	NOISY	QUIET	DELICATE	HARDY	CAGE	AVIARY
RED-CRESTED FINCH	*Coryphospingus cucullatus*	16cm (6.3in)		●	●			●
BLACK-CRESTED FINCH	*Lophospingus pusillus*	13cm (5in)		●	●			●
CINNAMON WARBLING FINCH	*Poospiza ornata*	13cm (5in)		●	●			●
RINGED WARBLING FINCH	*Poospiza torquata*	13cm (5in)		●	●			●
SAFFRON FINCH	*Sicalis flaveola*	14cm (5.5in)		●	●			●
BLUE-BLACK GRASSQUIT	*Volatina jacarina*	11cm (4.4in)		●	●			●
WHITE-COLLARED SEED-EATER	*Sporophila torqueola*	13cm (5in)		●	●			●
WHITE-THROATED SEED-EATER	*Sporophila albogularis*	10cm (4in)		●	●			●

NEW WORLD BUNTINGS

This group of buntings requires seed mixture 3 plus a little chopped fruit and green food, as well as insectivorous soft food and a few live insects.

Their cup-shaped nests are constructed of grasses, plant fibres, hair and feathers on a wicker or twig platform in dense shrub. Usually three or four eggs are laid, with incubation taking 13 days and fledging two weeks.

Lazuli Bunting

Orange-breasted Bunting

COMMON NAME	SCIENTIFIC NAME	SIZE	NOISY	QUIET	DELICATE	HARDY	CAGE	AVIARY
LAZULI BUNTING	*Passerina amoena*	13cm (5in)		●	●			●
INDIGO BUNTING	*Passerina cyanea*	13cm (5in)		●	●			●
VARIED BUNTING	*Passerina versicolor*	13cm (5in)		●	●			●
ORANGE-BREASTED BUNTING	*Passerina leclancherii*	14cm (5.5in)		●	●			●

CANARIES

Generations of intensive selective breeding have made today's canaries strikingly different from the wild parent stock on the Canary Islands. (The Romans named the Canary Islands *Canaria Insula* (Isle of Dogs) because they were inhabited by ferocious canines.)

The Wild Canary (*Serinus canaria*) is a relatively dull bird blessed with a melodious voice. From this humble ancestor, first kept solely for its song, has evolved an amazing diversity of form and colour. When canaries first arrived in Europe – and for several centuries thereafter, travel was extremely difficult and few people journeyed far from home. This meant that captive birds remained effectively isolated from all but their closest neighbours. Breeding within these separated populations soon caused characteristic plumage that distinguished them from the parent stock. It was not long before yellow mutants, heavily flecked with black, appeared among captive birds. Selective breeding from these led to the attractive yellow birds that most people today regard as the typical canary.

Selective breeding began in earnest around 1600 in Italy (from where birds were exported to Germany) and today the names of many varieties reflect their regional origins. Parisian Frill, German Crest, Lancashire Coppy, Gloster Corona – the names resonate with local pride and read like a gazetteer of Europe. To the Bernese, Padovan, Yorkshire, London, Norwich, Fife and Fiorino canaries can now be added Hoso and Makige from Japan and many more. Parallel to the breeding of birds for their physical features, German breeders were concentrating on the quality of song, a division that is still reflected in such names as Hartz and Timbrado.

The first comprehensive guide to the many different forms appeared in 1709. Written by the Duchesse du Barry's aviary superintendent, Hervieux, it recorded 29 varieties based upon differences in plumage. Since then, the number has multiplied into numerous 'types', known as Type Canaries. Variations in posture, feather structure and behaviour have led to new strains, while cross-breeding with the Black-hooded Red Siskin from South America has resulted in a whole new class of birds, the Coloured Canaries. At a recent show in the UK, prizes were awarded in over 100 different canary categories alone – and who knows what forms will emerge in the years ahead?

FEEDING MANAGEMENT

Young canaries learn where to find food from their parents, but once separated or introduced into a new environment, they may need help in locating feeding containers. A small amount of food sprinkled on the cage floor at the base of the container will act as a guide. Ideally, more than one feeder should be used when several birds are housed together and they should be placed conveniently near the perches. Avoid feeding birds in outside flights where seed can become damp and mouldy.

A large amount of seeds in an open container is easily fouled by droppings or can become damp when water is splashed on it. Unless the seed is well protected, offer no more than the daily requirement. Fouled seed is a source of trouble and should be removed, whether in a container or spread on the floor.

A guide to seed mixtures for canaries is given on pp64–65; otherwise buy a good canary mix. Ensure that fresh green food is available daily, and include vitamin and mineral supplements. Soaked seed is welcomed, especially when chicks are being reared.

ABOVE *Yellow-fronted Canary* (Serinus mozambicus)
TOP *A clear yellow hen, Border Canary*
BELOW *Canary feeding on fresh greenstuff*

TYPE CANARIES

BORDER FANCY

This graceful and active bird was developed in the Border country spanning England and Scotland during the 19th century. Since that time it has changed in size but few of its earlier characteristics of type, poise and posture have changed. Medium-sized, they should not exceed 14.6cm (5.8in) in length. Once a slimmer bird, today's show winners have well-rounded heads, along with a well-filled and rounded body. They make ideal pets and because they are reliable breeders are an obvious choice for the beginner.

LIZARD FANCY

One of the oldest breeds, first recorded in France at the beginning of the 18th century, it was developed to perfection during Georgian times when scientific minds were more at ease with the principles of heredity.

Lizards are judged for the moon-shaped, spangle markings over their back, a characteristic known to be in existence since 1709. Apart from improvements in colour, essential features of this fancy have not changed for almost 300 years. Brighter yellow birds are referred to as 'golds', buff birds as 'silver'.

GLOSTER FANCY

Glosters were developed from the Crested Roller and small Border canaries in the early 1920s. They are excellent exhibition birds, relatively easy to train and therefore another good choice for the novice exhibitors. The Plainhead is referred to as 'Consort' and the crested as 'Corona'.

Pairing crested birds produces the 'lethal factor' (see p131), therefore Coronas should only be paired with Consorts.

LANCASHIRE FANCY

The Lancashire Canary appears to have been created by pairing a Yorkshire with a Crested canary. This Fancy, thought to have originated in the 1850s, was at its prime some 30 years later and was typified by birds with small, oval-shaped heads and horseshoe-shaped crests. By the 1920s they had all but disappeared. Two main types were recognized, the Plainhead and the Crested, but there also existed a much larger variety, called the Lancashire Coppy.

FIFE FANCY

The Fife is a smaller version of the Border, 10.8cm (4.2in) in length. At competitions it is judged by almost identical rules, the emphasis being on size. It has to have a small, neat, spherical head with centrally positioned eyes, a nicely proportioned, compact egg-shaped body with firm, glossy plumage. Ideally it should sit semi-erect.

NORWICH FANCY

Norwich canaries have, in the past, been notorious for developing feather cysts, causing enthusiasts to turn to other varieties.

Good, clean Norwich stock became difficult to obtain, until a few dedicated breeders introduced the Cinnamon gene. Then, in the 1930s, the modern Norwich Plainhead was developed from a Border/Norwich cross and the cyst problem seems to have disappeared.

It was with a Norwich Canary that the effects of feeding with cayenne pepper first became apparent – and colour-feeding started. Bird-keepers, not realising that a brightly coloured plumage would develop, would administer the spice as a tonic to help the bird through its moult.

YORKSHIRE FANCY

The Yorkshire is one of the most difficult canaries to show-train, as it must have an erect posture. There must be no hint of a hunched appearance. This Fancy is thought to have developed in the late 1800s from Belgian and Lancashire fancies. Improvements in posture were sought during the 1930s by the introduction of Norwich blood.

THE SCOTS FANCY

The modern standard for the Scots Fancy is a long, half-moon-shaped body with a clean outline. This means short, tight feathering as opposed to the loose feathering of times past. Exhibition birds are required to be active and move freely between the perches of the show cage.

THE FRILLS

Frilled canaries are much more popular in Europe than the rest of the world – they probably originated there during the early part of the 19th century. The description of the 'Old Dutch' canary seems to tie in well with the birds we call Frills today: 'being ungainly to a degree; in position neither upright nor anything else; in feather rough, coarse and disorderly to an extent that cannot be equalled for slovenliness'. Another description of the Dutch Fancy around the same time suggested a large handsome bird with bold, erect and noble carriage, rough in body feather with heavy frilling to the back and breast. These birds were the likely forefathers of today's frills, from the tiny Gibber Italicus to the large and very recent Italian Giant Frill.

GIBBER ITALICUS

As this type of Frill exists only in a yellow feather type, it has suffered from persistent yellow to yellow pairings and deteriorations in plumage have become obvious. Many birds now lack feathering on the upper legs and breast.

THE ITALIAN GIANT FRILL

This giant is the largest of all canaries. Developed in northern Italy, some birds are as long as 25cm (10in). The minimum standard for showing is 21cm (8.3in) and it must have an erect posture of 60° or more.

The plumage is typically frilled, but unlike others its collar feathers are upturned towards the head. The collar meets up with the head feathering to form a substantial, rounded cask or hood.

PARISIAN FRILL

The upright stance along with good frill patterning and claws that twist like corkscrews are points that are judged in competition. At a maximum of 21cm (8.3in), this is one of the larger frills.

PADOVIAN FRILL

Originating from Padua in Italy, this Frill is also crested but resembles the Parisian in many ways, particularly the Plainhead variety. The Milan Frill is also similar, but Padovians lack the characteristic bouquet-shaped mantle end.

Intensive Red

*Gold
Brown Ino*

*Silver
Isabel*

*Recessive White
Agate Pastel*

COLOURED CANARIES

Coloured canaries require identical bird-keeping skills to those required for Type canaries, and an easily managed breeding system goes a long way to achieving good results.

The confusion between different nomenclatures adopted by early breeders has made it difficult to follow the profusion of names, but today a more unified approach is being adopted. Different mutations that have appeared in the past, such as the Opal, Pastel, Ino and Satinette, continue to play an important part in the fancy. Other, more recent mutations are known as Topaz, Onyx and Eumo. With the popularity of this branch of bird-keeping, we can expect more to follow.

FEATHER TYPES

There are three feather types for Coloured canaries. The 'Intensive', equivalent to the Yellow in Type canaries, and the 'Non-intensive', equivalent to the Buff. Intensive feathers are narrower than Non-intensive feathers. A third feather type, the 'Dimorphic', is much broader than the Non-intensive.

COLOURS

Three lipochrome colours are possible – Red, Gold, White and Silver. Combining these colours with the ivory factor produces Rose, Gold Ivory and White Ivory respectively. Recessive White, which comes within the white lipochrome colour, cannot be combined to produce different colours.

Coloured canaries can be divided into two more categories – the Clear and Selfs.

Clear

Clear, ticked and variegated birds can be bred as Intensive, Non-intensive and Dimorphic in Red, Rose, Gold and Gold Ivory. Also in this category are the dominant and recessive white birds in clear, ticked or variegated shades.

*Dimorphic Clear
Red hen*

Selfs

This group of canaries has a dark-coloured underflue (background) and patterned markings. Selfs can be divided into two series: 'Classics' and 'Non-classics'.

The Classic series of Selfs includes Blue, Green, Bronze, Brown (or Cinnamon), Isabel and Agate. The Non-classic series includes Ino, Opal, Pastel, Topaz, Onyx, Eumo and Satinette.

It is possible to breed all Selfs in all three feather types as well as the lipochrome colours. The Satinette occurs only as an Agate or Isabel, with the remainder occurring in all the Classic series.

*Red-bronze
cock*

Rose Isabel

*Dimorphic Red
Opal cock*

INO

Ino birds have red eyes. Both Green and Brown series Inos have feathers edged and tipped with a rich dark brown. Ideally, they must show as a pattern of scalloped lines over the whole plumage. Agate and Isabel Ino birds frequently appear as clear lipochrome specimens.

Rose Brown Ino

OPAL

Opal birds have dark steel-grey-coloured striations on a lipochrome-coloured background. In Agate-series Opal birds, the striations are much narrower than in the Green-series Opal. Brown-series Opal patterning is suffused over the head and flanks but shows as a spangling on the back. Isabel Opal birds appear as a dilute version of the Brown Opal.

Intensive Gold Opal Agate hen

Dimorphic Rose Bronze Opal

GREEN (GREYWING) AND PASTEL

The markings on Green birds are charcoal-grey in colour with a deep lipochrome coloured background. Pastel Green-series birds have straight striations on the flanks and upper breast, but show only a slight spangled pattern on the back.

Pastel Brown-series birds have very indistinct striations, appearing a suffused brown colour overall. Pastel Isabel birds are similar, but appear as dilute Pastel Browns. The Pastel Agate has fine markings over most of its body except on the belly.

SATINETTES

All Satinettes have red eyes. Isabel Satinettes show unbroken, fine, brown striations extending from the bill over the crown and back to the rump and also from the flanks into the upper breast. These should be backed by deep lipochrome coloration. Agate Satinettes show only faint markings, appearing almost as Clear birds.

TOPAZ

This mutation is closely related to the Ino. Green and Agate Topaz birds show dark charcoal-grey striations along the feather quill that create a striking pattern, particularly in the Agate and Dimorphic series.

ONYX

Closely related to the Opal is the Onyx. However, the Onyx produces more melanin, giving it a darker appearance. Green-series Onyx birds have black striations and a dark suffusion.

EUMO

The Eumo has red eyes. As the brown suffusion is suppressed, these birds appear very bright as the clear lipochrome colour shows through the striated patterning.

Brown series Eumo birds have rich dark-brown striations giving them the appearance of Classic Isabels.

Silver Blue Greywing Pastel

Non-intensive Gold Agate Pastel

Clear Gold Satinette (non show bird)

Recessive Silver Isabel

SINGING CANARIES

Singing canaries are judged on their song, not their looks. Yet they are not unattractive and do not lack the qualities of breeding apportioned to the Type canaries. Even to the extreme of, say a deformed bird without feathers, as long as it has the ability to sing well it stands a chance in a competition. In continental Europe, the Singing Canary Fancy is represented by the Hartz and Timbrado as well as the Roller Canary, but elsewhere the Roller alone seems to be more prevalent.

Singing canaries are available in many colours. The modern Roller Canary, for instance, appears in Greens, Yellows, Variegated, Dominant Whites, Dominant Blue, Green Opal, Silver-Blue Opal and Orange.

Anyone interested in singing canaries needs first to get in touch with one of the many clubs specialising in this branch of the fancy. Obtaining birds that perform well can be a bit daunting, as contesting breeders hold on to their young birds until such a time that they prove their ability to sing. Although the best birds are seldom for sale, it is possible to obtain youngsters related to them. The song of young birds does not develop into that recognized as true Roller song for at least a few months after weaning, so autumn, the time when young cocks are put into training, is the best time to obtain stock. The clubs are a good place to start and champion breeders will invariably give help to the newcomer.

Keeping Roller canaries for their song is a decision not to be taken lightly, as it can restrict other bird-keeping activities. Housing Singing canaries within earshot of other species, and especially other canaries, will inevitably destroy their song and their ability to perform in competition. They will pick up phrases of song from other species often intermixed with their own.

Whereas most bird shows are visual exhibitions of form and plumage, singing competitions rely totally on the sound of the bird's voice and its ability to perform recognised phrases. The birds are kept in the dark in special cages with hinged doors closed across the front until it is their turn to perform in front of the judges. The cages are brought together in small groups, usually four at a time, and the doors opened so simulating daybreak and encouraging the birds' natural tendency to sing. A certain amount of prompting is often necessary – the trainer's tool of a few small pebbles in a matchbox produces a rattling sound. Eventually, the birds start to sing their phrases with the judge marking them on their abilities.

Points are awarded on the quality of their performance, recognised in terms such as 'Rolls' and 'Tours'. These characteristics are further subdivided into song phrases with names like 'Hollow Roll', 'Water Glucke Tour' and 'Schockel', all names reminiscent of the heartland of Singing canaries in central Europe. Winners of each round are then set to perform against each other until an overall winner is established.

ABOVE *Singing canaries are trained in simulated dawn-light conditions.* BELOW *The canary is kept in darkness just before judging. When the doors are opened the bird begins to sing, as it assumes it is early morning.*

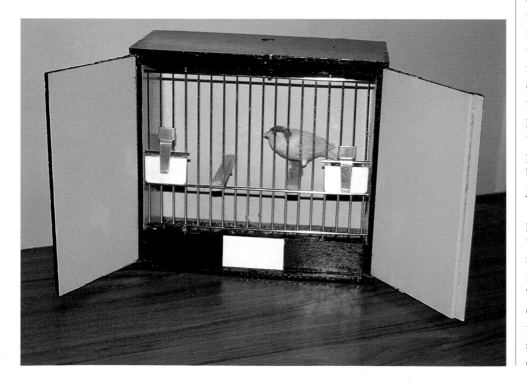

DOMESTICATED MUTATIONS

In recent years, domesticated colourful mutations of many species have been bred by fanciers, to create a whole new array of colourful birds. For generations, the budgerigar was really the only species able to be bred in a large number of coloured varieties. Although new types of budgerigars continue to appear, other species are catching up on the trend.

Coloured canaries are being produced in brighter hues, but the range of colours is not changing greatly. Breeders are also concentrating their efforts on many other parrot-like species – none more so than the cockatiels, lovebirds and parakeets. Australian finches are also available in many different coloured mutations, with the brightly coloured Gouldian Finch now being produced looking like an artist's palette.

Lineolated Parakeet
(Bolborhynchus lineola)
(Lutino mutation)

Perhaps it is the challenge of creating different varieties that is the driving force, but the commercial aspect must always play some part in this pastime. There is always competition to produce something new that will be outstanding and hence in demand by others. It is now being realised that this trend has more disadvantages than ever anticipated, for it is becoming difficult with several species to obtain aviary-bred normal coloured birds. Species like the Gouldian Finch and Java Sparrow are typical examples. What is more alarming is that the wild populations of these species are becoming uncommon, and should aviary-bred stock be required for conservation purposes, they will just not be available. The serious aviculturist should realise this possibility and endeavour to maintain a stock of healthy, normal birds.

Ring-necked Parakeet (Psittacula krameri)
(Blue mutation)

1　　　　2　　　　3　　　　4　　　　5

LEFT TO RIGHT: *1 and 2. Gouldian Finch mutations* (Chloebia gouldiae) *3. Turquoise Grass Parakeet* (Neophema pulchella) *(Yellow mutation)*
4. Peach-faced Lovebird (Pastel Blue mutation) 5. Bourkes Parrot (Neophema bourkii) *(Rosa mutation)*

BUDGERIGARS

ABOVE *Colonial nesting of budgerigars in aviaries is frequently unsuccessful due to disturbance by non-breeding birds.*
BELOW *Play with your budgerigars regularly and they will become quite tame.*

The Wild Budgerigar, or Shell Parakeet (*Melopsittacus undulatus*), originates from the arid regions of Australia and is pale grass-green in colour. It was first brought to Europe in 1840 by the naturalist and wildlife artist John Gould. A few years later, breeding was established in Germany and France.

Today, the species is well domesticated and has become a favourite exhibition bird with numerous varieties in colour and markings. The Yellow mutation was easily developed as it already existed in wild populations. Around 1890, the first Blue mutations were bred in Belgium and France, and White varieties, although not pure white, followed soon thereafter.

As late as 1932, the first Albino appeared in Germany, and the Lutino at around the same time. New colours and different patterning are continually developed, presenting a wide choice for delightfully coloured pets or avicultural specimens.

The budgerigar is, probably, the most adaptable of all the parrotlike birds, taking to a cage where most others of the family will settle only in aviaries. Its tame, confiding manner and ability to mimic have made it a favourite pet and the most popular parakeet on the market. If it is well cared for, it can live for up to 12 years.

HOUSING

When space is limited, a budgerigar is the obvious choice, but, like all birds, it needs space to stretch its wings and have an opportunity to fly each day. The minimum recommended cage size for one or two birds is 60cm x 30cm x 40cm (24in x 12in x 16in). Indoor aviaries are excellent, especially if more than one bird is to be kept. However, do not be tempted to overcrowd them.

As with most parrotlike birds, budgerigars are destructive – an aviary bare of plants is advised. All that is needed is an ample supply of perches in different shapes and sizes, set at various heights and spaced so that droppings do not fall in water or food containers, or on any birds perched lower down.

FEEDING

A guide to seed mixtures for small parakeets is given on p65 – otherwise choose a good proprietary mix. Ensure that fresh green food is available every day. Except when pre-packed budgerigar seed mixes are fed, vitamin and mineral supplements may be necessary to prevent deficiencies. A feeding regime similar to that advised for canaries should be adopted.

At the start of the breeding season, it is essential that birds are brought into peak breeding condition, and additional nutriment is advised. A weekly supplement of oats sprinkled with glucose powder and well mixed with a little olive oil gets them off to a good start.

BREEDING

A standard breeding cage, set aside in the living room, will normally provide a draught-proof enclosure and you may even be successful with a breeding pair, provided there is no undue disturbance. Standard nest boxes, which fix onto the front of breeding cages, are widely available.

When more than a pair are kept for breeding purposes, the bird room is the obvious choice. Budgerigars tend to make a mess and there is invariably a lot of fine dust. A normal bird room, well ventilated with plenty of daylight is sufficient to start. Non-breeding birds should be kept in separate flights, males in one and females in another. Young birds can also benefit by being kept separate from adults. Breeding budgerigars need a regular lighting regime for the greatest success. Successful breeders have found that splitting the day into two light periods with a twilight zone in the middle of the day is very effective. Six hours of artificial light in the bird room, starting early in the morning followed by a couple of hours with the lights off, allows the birds a 'rest-period' in the middle of the day. The light can then be on again for another eight or so hours throughout the afternoon and evening. This lighting sequence is easily arranged by means of an automatic time switch of which there are many types available on the market.

Many breeders advocate all-wire breeding cages set in tiers. Between each row is a sheet of plastic or metal to catch the droppings and seed husks. Cleaning is so simple – you simply remove the separating sheet, which can be scraped clean and easily washed. Any bits that falls to the ground are easily swept up or collected in a vacuum cleaner. Nest boxes can be very light – 6mm (1/4in) plywood is adequate – and these can be hung on the

Breeding budgerigars is a fascinating and fun-filled hobby, which can lead to more ambitious ventures in colour.

Cobalt (cock)

Cinnamon Light Green (cock)

Spangle White/ Grey (hen)

Skyblue Pied (cock)

Lutino (hen)

Albino (cocks)

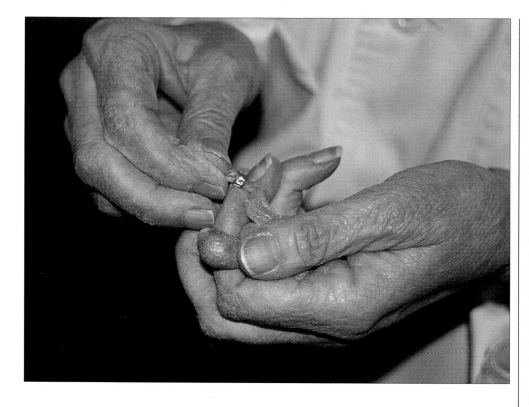

Ringing a baby budgerigar, to provide proof of its date of birth.

Yellow Double Factor Spangle (hen)

front of the cage by simple hooks. If spare boxes are kept, cleaning becomes particularly easy, as the chicks can be transferred to a clean box without the parents noticing much of a change.

If you wish to keep track of the parentage of chicks, breeding cages set up in a bird room are advised; where this is not important, an aviary is sufficient. A colony of breeding budgerigars in an aviary is an attractive sight, but ensure that the birds are well-paired to avoid disagreements and bickering among them. Ensure that all nest boxes hang at the same height, otherwise they will fight to occupy the highest one. A purpose-built row of nests with separating screens protruding from the front between the openings will overcome this problem.

Still, whatever precautions you take, there will invariably be some birds that are more aggressive than others and the aviary needs to be monitored carefully.

A normal clutch consists of four or five eggs, but eight or more are also possible. The hen incubates her eggs for 18 days and the

fledglings leave the nest after about five weeks. After fledging, the young should be feeding themselves in around seven days, when they must be moved to other accommodation to prevent interference with any second clutch of eggs that may follow.

BREEDING PROBLEMS

Like most of domesticated species, budgerigars seem prone to problems during the breeding season. Fortunately most of them can be overcome, often relying on old tried and tested solutions. To the novice, these problems often occur right from the start, at the egg stage. It is at this time that parent birds are at their most vulnerable and need to be in tip-top breeding condition. Inexperienced parents may also be under stress, and we should not really expect everything to go without some mishap.

Eggs fail for several different reasons – perhaps the most common is fertility. A fertile egg has a nice, shiny, opaque white shell, which when held up to the light shows the developing embryo as a red spot and veins. Do not over-handle the eggs, as this can lead to dead-in-shell chicks or even the eggs becoming addled.

Infertility may be caused by several factors, yet a few obvious but often overlooked reasons may need addressing.

- The mating of cock and hen may not be successful because the perch is insecure or round and smooth, so preventing proper contact.
- Similarly, with inexperienced and immature birds, the hen fails to raise her tail properly or the cock misses the target.
- Some hens spend so much time in the nest box that copulation cannot ever take place.

Once eggs are laid they may be damaged by puncturing by claws. The immediate and often successful solution is to paint over and seal the hole with a quick-drying nail varnish. Trimming the hen's toenails can stop it from happening again.

Addled eggs occur when a fertile egg has failed to develop properly and the chick has died. The egg then appears a dirty grey in colour. The most common reason for this is the eggs getting chilled when the hen leaves them for extended periods, particularly at night. Other reasons may be nonviable eggs due to a failure of the parents diet to provide sufficient nutrients prior to egg-laying, or the chick may be carrying a lethal gene.

The diet of the parents may cause weakness within the chick, and so prevent it from breaking out of the shell. This problem, known as 'dead-in-shell', may also be caused by low humidity. Low humidity can cause the egg to become drier at its surface, which affects the membrane around the chicks – the membrane becomes inelastic and tough and traps the baby bird.

Soft-shelled eggs can be caused by lack of calcium in the diet or a failure of the shell-forming process. If you find such eggs, remove them.

Curing the calcium deficiency may be achieved by adding 20% solution of calcium borogluconate at the rate of 1ml (0.034 fl oz) to one litre (1 fl pint) of the drinking water.

Sometimes eggs will be eaten soon after they are laid. The reason for this is unknown, but usually put down to inexperience by the hen. Any broken eggs should be removed as soon as possible. If the hen is young she will usually lay again and go on to incubate perfectly normally. If it becomes a problem, though, there are two popular solutions.

Firstly, it may be possible to train the hen to accept the eggs: salvage any eggs and replace them with a marble. While she is attempting to attack the marble, you will hear it rolling around. Once the rolling sound ceases and she begins to sit on the marble, replace her own eggs. Hopefully she will carry on naturally.

If this fails, place a soft pad beneath a small hole in the base of the nest pan; the eggs will fall through onto the pad. Collect them and incubate them under a foster hen or a purpose-built incubator.

The sex of an adult budgerigar is easily determined from the colour of its cere, the fleshy protuberance at the base of the beak. In healthy males, this is usually blue, while in females it is brown. In young budgerigars and in types such as the lutinos and albinos, male bird's ceres are a pinkish-purple. In all young males, however, the colour is usually darker and more purple. Another way to tell the age of a budgie is that young birds have all-dark irises, lacking the white iris of adults.

Breeding budgerigars is a fascinating hobby – and often leads to more ambitious ventures. It is therefore wise to keep good records establishing the parentage of any birds in the stud at the earliest possible time. Do not include only variety and colour – also note whether they were good parents, for example. Computer software is available to make record-keeping easy: one of the best on the market is 'Birdstud', which is simple to use yet thorough in its purpose.

There is plenty of information on budgerigars, with numerous books available and some good sites on the Internet. Try Budgerigars Galore (www.budgerigars.co.uk), with more than 370 pages packed with information.

Light Green Spangle

Opaline Suffused Yellow

Dark-green Dominant Pied (cock)

Violet (cock)

THE ART OF BREEDING

ABOVE *A conveniently sited nest box in an outdoor aviary.*
TOP *Nest baskets.*

Until the middle of the 19th century, few exotic animals survived transportation from their countries of origin. The trauma of the long sea voyages took a particularly heavy toll on delicate creatures such as birds, and any that were still alive at the end of the journey were sold as pets and not given the correct conditions in which to breed. The one notable exception was the canary, which has been bred across Europe since the early 15th century.

As travel became easier and faster, the number of live birds arriving from distant lands increased dramatically, with the result that selling prices dropped and bird-keeping became widely popular. Yet for many years breeding was not considered viable and the demand for cage birds continued to be satisfied by capturing wild specimens; exotic imports remained in demand even though the mortality rate was high.

Human pressure has gravely reduced the size of wild populations, driving some species to the brink of extinction. Consequently, strict regulations are now enforced to reduce the traffic in wild-caught birds. Many countries, such as Australia, severely restrict all bird imports and exports, while international agreements prohibit – at least in theory – trade in endangered and protected species.

Today, the only way in which many of the desirable species can be made available to bird lovers is through captive breeding. In fact, captive breeding and release programmes have turned the tide, and the conservation of many species is becoming dependent on the knowledge gained by bird-keepers.

Recent years have seen a steady increase in captive-bred species that were previously considered endangered. For example, well over three-quarters of known parrot species are now being bred in captivity, which bodes well for their wild relatives.

Both male and female Blackbirds (Turdus merula) *share the responsibility of rearing their young.*

Breeding, therefore, is not only rewarding and fascinating in its own right – it also contributes to the conservation of wild bird populations by making their capture unnecessary and unprofitable. For the novice, simply keeping birds is usually challenge enough, but the experienced aviculturist may discover that the greatest reward is to be found in breeding.

Budgerigars, in particular, offer a challenge to the bird-keeper, for it is not the species in itself that is the attraction but the potentially huge variety of colours that can be produced through breeding.

Cockatiels, lovebirds, Australian finches, Grass Parakeets, quail, doves and Java Sparrows are all undergoing similar experimentation to produce new colour forms. Nevertheless, it is important to keep part of your aviary-bred stock free from mutation, as it is this bank of genetic material that becomes available to restock wild populations when they become endangered.

Zebra Finch and Chestnut-flanked White.

DNA tests require that either a freshly plucked breast feather or a small drop of blood from the bird be sent to a pathology laboratory specializing in avian sexing techniques. The procedure is inexpensive and extremely simple; a sampling kit is usually provided by the laboratory.

Before the advent of DNA testing, sexing was done by laparotomy (surgical sexing). This technique involved making a tiny incision, under anaesthetic, to facilitate an inspection of the bird's internal sex organs. Whereas male birds have symmetrical sex organs with paired testes and *vasa deferentia*, females are highly asymmetrical, with the right ovary and its associated structures totally suppressed. Only the left ovary is present, and a trained veterinary surgeon can easily see this condition through an endoscope – a slender viewing device that can be inserted through a small slit in the body wall.

The male Blue-breasted Quail (Cotumix chinensis) has rather flamboyant plumage, while the female is drab in colour.

SEXING

Before any selective breeding can take place it is obviously necessary to determine the sex of the available stock.

In many species this presents little difficulty, as the cock is immediately recognized by his more flamboyant plumage. However, there are numerous species in which the sexes are visually indistinguishable and alternative methods of recognition must be used.

The methods most likely to dominate in the near future are based on DNA samples. These require microscopic examination of living cells to determine the number of sex chromosomes (if only a single Y chromosome is present, the bird is a hen). The chief advantage of these techniques, apart from the fact that they are noninvasive, very safe and almost 100 per cent accurate, is that they can be done immediately after hatching and do not require waiting until the bird matures. This allows the breeder to devote space and attention only to those individuals needed for future crosses.

The nuclei of all living cells contain chromosomes, each consisting of two strands joined together about their halfway point. They appear under the microscope as very fine threads and are in identical looking pairs. The chromosome contains genes arranged along its length like a string of beads. Each gene controls a specific characteristic, although certain characteristics may be controlled by several genes acting together. When a cell divides, the chromosomes must behave in an orderly way so that the genes are divided equally.

In the 1950s the structure of the DNA molecule was discovered by working out the positions of various atoms in the molecule. It can be represented as in the diagram by a double helix joined together by bars like the rungs of a ladder. The 'rungs' are made up of pairs of organic bases, of which there are four types.

The order in which these bases are arranged forms a series that is variable and that controls how the genes exert their influence on the organism. In effect, the DNA contains a full set of instructions (the genetic code) responsible for the way an organism develops.

Genetics

Natural selection, the basis of evolution, is dependent on two key elements:

- the competition for survival and successful reproduction
- the offspring of any mating are not identical but exhibit slight variation.

In essence, if one variant gains advantage over the other for reproductive success, this advantage is more likely to be passed on to future generations. The less advantageous variant, likewise, will gradually be eliminated from the population. The aviculturist, through skillful breeding, is able to subvert the short-term course of evolution to his or her own ends by influencing both the nature of the variation and the selection that acts upon it.

Characteristics passed on from parent to offspring are coded within the reproductive cells – the sperm and egg – in the form of amino acid sequences that are contained on DNA strands in the cell nucleus. These are called chromosomes. Each characteristic is controlled by one or more genes, which are specific regions of the chromosome containing particular fragments of DNA code. The

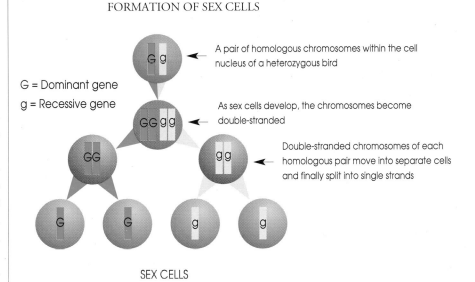

FORMATION OF SEX CELLS

G = Dominant gene
g = Recessive gene

A pair of homologous chromosomes within the cell nucleus of a heterozygous bird

As sex cells develop, the chromosomes become double-stranded

Double-stranded chromosomes of each homologous pair move into separate cells and finally split into single strands

SEX CELLS

processes involved in sexual reproduction ensure that each developing egg receives a mixture of genes from both parents, but in widely differing combinations. The science of genetics determines which of the characteristics are inherited.

Typically, each chromosome in a cell belongs to a matched pair, except those that determine sex which are single. However, reproductive sperm and egg cells are produced with unpaired chromosomes, and the full complement is restored as the cells unite at fertilization.

A chick receives one set of chromosomes from each parent. This means that each character trait is carried in a pair of genes, one lying on the chromosome from each parent. However, the members of each gene pair need not be identical. From time to time small changes may occur in the coding. These are called mutations, and come about through a variety of causes, including cosmic radiation (electromagnetic radiation from outer space) and abnormal physical change during replication. While some mutations are profoundly disruptive and inevitably fatal as will be described later, others are essentially benign and affect such characteristics as feather shape, colour, patterning or size. These can be assimilated and perpetuated by selective breeding.

LEFT *A newly hatched Fischer's Lovebird* (Agapornis fischeri).

GENETIC RULES

The genetic rules were formulated by an Austrian monk named Gregor Mendel during the 1870s, although his meticulously detailed work remained unrecognized for years. It was long after Mendel's death in 1884 that the mechanisms of inheritance underlying his observations were finally understood.

Mendel's work involved the observation of inheritance traits in garden peas (*Pisum sativum*) which can reproduce in a relatively short time. He chose the pea for its easily controlled fertilization – and accidental fertilization was almost impossible. Concentrating on the individual contrasting traits he was able to cross tall with short as well as contrasting colours. The progeny were clearly identified and used to trace breeding results through subsequent generations, so developing a set of statistical rules.

Resulting from his experiments he concluded that 'discrete hereditary elements'(now known as genes) held within the sex cells are responsible for the transmission of traits.

When an individual carries identical genes on each of a pair of chromosomes, it is said to be homozygous. When the genes differ the individual is said to be heterozygous (see the illustration below).

Among bird-keepers, heterozygous individuals are commonly referred to as 'split'. It is very important to understand that when an individual is split for a particular character, say green or blue feather colour, there is no blending or mixing. Each form remains true and will be transmitted to subsequent generations in predictable proportions. A heterozygous, or split individual will carry genetic material for both alleles (alternative manifestations of either green or blue feathers) but, of course, it can appear only as one or the other. In this case the form that consistently appears in the first (F1) generation will be said to be dominant, while its partner is called recessive and will manifest only in subsequent generations. Most mutations affecting colour in birds are recessive.

COMBINATION OF SEX CELLS AT
FERTILIZATION

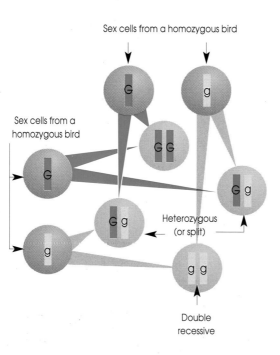

Sex cells from a homozygous bird

Sex cells from a homozygous bird

Heterozygous (or split)

Double recessive

THE CHROMOSOMES

In most animal cells, be they birds, mammals or fruit flies, there are two types of chromosomes. One pair, 'the sex chromosomes', determine the sex of the individual. The remainder, called 'autosomes', of which there can be as many as 60 pairs, determine all other characteristics. In humans, the chromosomes that determine sex are conventionally designated X and Y and behave somewhat differently to the rest. X chromosomes carry large numbers of genes, while Y chromosomes are much shorter and bear less genetic information.

In other animals the convention may sometimes be different. For instance, birds' sex chromosomes are normally designated Z and Y but differ from humans in that males possess two Z chromosomes (ZZ) and females one Z and one Y (ZY).

The normal way in which chromosomes split is called mitosis; it is simply a method of duplication. However, in the production of sperm and eggs (within the male or female body), the process is different. Called meiosis, it ensures that sperm and egg contain only half the normal complement of genetic material.

When a hen produces egg cells by meiosis, all possess one of each type of autosomal chromosome plus one Z chromosome. Hence, all her eggs are alike in chromosome content. When the cock produces sperm cells, each sperm will contain a set of autosomes, but half will have a Z and the other half a Y chromosome. The result is that, at fertilization, half the zygotes (combined sperm and egg cells) will be ZY (female) and the other half ZZ (male).

Since hens have sex chromosomes of different length, and there is only one gene to consider, she cannot be split as there is no corresponding gene on the opposite short Y chromosome. For this reason her appearance (phenotype) and genetic make-up (genotype) are very similar. Recessive mutations carried on the Z chromosomes are therefore said to be sex-linked and inherited somewhat differently to autosomal recessives.

In order that maximum numbers of sex-linked mutant offspring are produced, pairing with cocks of the desired colour increases the number of mutant chicks when paired with normal hens. Among the budgerigars that follow this pattern are Cinnamons, Opalines, Lutinos, Albinos and Lacewings; among the Cockatiels: Lutino, Pearl and Cinnamon.

SEX-LINKED PAIRING AND OFFSPRING						
PARENTS			**CHICKS**			
COCK		HEN	COCKS		HENS	
SEX-LINKED	X	NORMAL	50% NORMAL/SEX-LINKED		50% SEX-LINKED	
NORMAL	X	SEX-LINKED	50% NORMAL/SEX-LINKED		50% NORMAL	
SEX-LINKED	X	SEX-LINKED	50% SEX-LINKED		50% SEX-LINKED	
NORMAL/SEX-LINKED	X	NORMAL	25% NORMAL	25% NORMAL/SEX-LINKED	25% NORMAL	25% SEX-LINKED
NORMAL/SEX-LINKED	X	SEX-LINKED	25% NORMAL/SEX-LINKED	25% SEX-LINKED	25% NORMAL	25% SEX-LINKED

CROSSES

Cross-breeding birds with different genetic mutations results in progeny having genetic make-up (genotype) in accordance with Mendel's basic laws of genetics, but it should be stressed that the percentages discussed here are not absolute but a statistical average.

The physical appearance (phenotype) can be misleading, as it is possible to have two individuals of the same phenotype but differing in genotype. We therefore need to establish, as close as possible, the genotypes of any pairing if we are to predict the outcome with any degree of reliability.

Recessive gene mutations

The natural colour of budgerigars in the wild is green, but there is a common recessive mutant form that is blue. These can be represented as G (for the dominant green gene) and g (for the recessive blue gene). When a pair of homozygous green budgerigars (GG) mate, all the offspring will, of course, be pure green too. Likewise, homozygous blue budgerigars (gg) will produce all pure blue offspring.

But what of other possible combinations? Take a pair of green birds, one of which is homozygous (GG) and the other is heterozygous (Gg). While the offspring will all be green, 50 per cent will be homozygous (GG) and 50 per cent heterozygous (Gg).

There exists just one further possible mating combination, which is of considerable practical significance. If a blue homozygous (gg) bird is crossed with a green heterozygous (Gg) one, the offspring will appear to be half-blue and half-green. The blue offspring will, of course, be (gg) homozygotes but the greens will all be (Gg) heterozygotes.

Cage bird mutation: Cinnamon Pearl Pied Cockatiel.

Cinnamon Grey hen.

RECESSIVE PAIRING AND OFFSPRING				
PARENT BIRDS			**CHICKS**	
RECESSIVE	X	NORMAL	100% NORMAL/RECESSIVE	
RECESSIVE	X	RECESSIVE	100% RECESSIVE	
RECESSIVE	X	NORMAL/RECESSIVE	50% RECESSIVE	50% NORMAL/RECESSIVE
NORMAL/RECESSIVE	X	NORMAL	50% NORMAL	50% NORMAL/RECESSIVE
NORMAL/RECESSIVE	X	NORMAL/RECESSIVE	50% NORMAL/RECESSIVE	25% NORMAL / 25% RECESSIVE

Skyblue Spangle cock.

White Double Factor Spangle cock.

Opaline Cinnamon Skyblue Spangle.

It is impossible to distinguish between Normal (homozygous) green and Split (heterozygous) green by looking at them, but if you are seeking to raise blue offspring and possess only one blue bird, this last cross will ensure that 50 per cent of the chicks will be blue when one parent is green.

Dominant gene mutations

Apart from the commonly occurring recessive genes, there are also a few unique mutations that are dominant. Since dominant traits are always manifest they cannot be split. Instead, heterozygotes are said to be Single Factor (sf) and homozygotes Double Factor (df), and it is generally impossible to distinguish between them by simple inspection.

The one exception to this rule involves the 'dark' gene of budgerigars and other parakeets, which affects the hue and saturation of their colour. When present on just one gene (sf), the effect is less pronounced than when present on both (df). Thus green birds are either dark green or olive, and blue birds, cobalt or mauve respectively.

DOMINANT PAIRING AND OFFSPRING

In order to breed a range of colours, it is important to understand how the progeny of dominant recessives differs with crosses of various parental types. Referring to the table below and using the Dominant Pied factor of budgerigars as an example, there are five possible combinations:

- Dominant Pied (sf) with Normal gives half Normal and half Dominant Pied (sf).
- Crossing two Dominant Pied (sf) individuals yields 50 per cent Dominant Pied (sf), 25 per cent Dominant Pied (df) and 25 per cent Normal.
- Dominant Pied (df) crossed with Normal produces 100 per cent Dominant Pied (sf) offspring.
- When Dominant Pied (df) and (sf) are crossed, the offspring are half (df) and half (sf).
- Crossing two Dominant Pied (df) individuals gives all Dominant Pieds (df).

The pattern into which particular traits are sorted will be different when their genes are carried on the sex chromosomes that determine gender. To show what happens, consider the common sex-linked recessive Lutino mutation in cockatiels. Remember that, because the hen has only a single sex chromosome, she cannot be Split for this trait, so that hens always show their genetic make-up (genotype).

- Pairing a Lutino cock with a Lutino hen results in all Lutino young, half male and half female.
- When a Normal cock crosses with a Lutino hen the offspring are half Normal hens and half Split cocks.
- Conversely, when a Lutino cock is crossed with a Normal hen, half the offspring are Lutino hens and half Split cocks. This type of cross is of particular significance to those wishing to breed such mutations as all the young can be used to propagate Lutino individuals.
- A Normal hen that has been mated with a Split cock will yield 25 per cent Normal cocks, 25 per cent Split cocks, 25 per cent Normal hens and 25 per cent Lutino hens.
- A Lutino hen that has been mated with a Split cock will yield 25 per cent split cocks, 25 per cent Lutino cocks, 25 per cent Normal hens and 25 per cent Lutino hens.

DOMINANT PAIRING AND OFFSPRING						
PARENT BIRDS				CHICKS		
SINGLE FACTOR	X	NORMAL	→	50% SINGLE FACTOR	50% NORMAL	
SINGLE FACTOR	X	SINGLE FACTOR	→	50% SINGLE FACTOR	25% NORMAL	25% DOUBLE FACTOR
DOUBLE FACTOR	X	NORMAL	→	100% SINGLE FACTOR		
DOUBLE FACTOR	X	SINGLE FACTOR	→	50% SINGLE FACTOR	50% DOUBLE FACTOR	
DOUBLE FACTOR	X	DOUBLE FACTOR	→	100% DOUBLE FACTOR		

The lethal factor

Lethal factors are mutant genes that can survive only in Split, or heterozygous individuals. When carried on both chromosomes of a pair, the embryo fails to develop properly and dies before hatching.

The genes that produce crested forms in budgerigars, canaries and a variety of other finches are such mutant genes, because the crest gene is carried on both chromosomes – homozygotes. The crested gene results from a dominant autosomal mutation.

The breeder wishing to perpetuate the crested strain should only mate Crested individuals (sf) with Normals, which will result in half Crested (sf) and half Normal offspring. If Crested birds are mated with one another, 25 per cent of the offspring will be nonviable homozygotes.

The theory of genetics and bird-breeding is often daunting to first-time bird-keepers, but the Internet can provide tremendous help for those in doubt. In fact, there are a number of computer software programmes available that can be invaluable in predicting the outcome of crosses. One such an example is the BUDGEN software, which can predict the resultant form from any combination of budgerigar colour cross without the user requiring any knowledge of genetic theory. Details of this and other useful bird-keeping software are available from http://www.2.tpg.com.au/users/kyorkc/.

LEFT *Circular-crest Opaline Skyblue cock.*
BELOW *An all-wire cage breeding bird room.*

BREEDING PRACTICALITIES

Breeding is perhaps the most critical period in a bird's life and the bird-keeper must ensure the best possible care and conditions if breeding is to succeed. The birds must be in peak health and condition. A significant factor is adequate nutrition, which will affect the birds' general health at a time when all their reserves are tested to the limit. Many require a change in diet and should be offered additional supplementary foods along with twigs of shooting buds and germinated seed.

When birds are ready to breed, their normal behaviour changes. They begin displaying, carrying nesting material and searching for a prospective site for their nest.

The bird-keeper's early preparation for breeding is essential to avoid disturbance during the early stages of pairing and the defining of territories. This applies particularly to wild species in aviaries rather than domesticated cage birds. Make sure all aviary plants are already well established and that all maintenance on the structure is complete. When the weather is appropriate, introduce nest boxes and platforms; for some species, though, such as many of the parrotlike species, it is essential to leave nest boxes in the aviary throughout the year for roosting purposes.

While many species will breed in large aviaries or flights, small, specially designed breeding cages are preferred for birds raised for exhibition purposes, particularly in domesticated types where proven parentage is important.

ABOVE A typical hole-type nest box to be placed in the aviary or cage.
RIGHT Male Chinese Painted Quail (black) and female Silver Quail Mutation tend to their eggs on the floor of an aviary. The hatchlings will be no larger than bumble bees.
BELOW Tiny Song Thrushes (Turdus Philomelos) await food from their parents.

NESTING

Appropriate nesting facilities must be provided within the breeding enclosure. These can range from sturdy nest boxes to wicker baskets, open trays or 'pans' for canaries. Many birds show strong preferences, choosing quiet locations that are well concealed from view, while others prefer to nest openly on the ground amid sand and pebbles. The more domesticated species will make nests in artificial nest boxes, while others prefer to construct their own.

Nest building is usually a conspicuous activity, soon followed by laying. At this time, one bird of the pair will probably be spending much of its time at the nest. Many non-domesticated species become particularly susceptible to disturbance at this time and care should be taken to minimize noise and disturbance of any kind. In mixed aviaries, territorial disputes can become a particular concern during breeding and early preparations need to be made to separate troublesome birds before nesting is underway.

The bird-keeper's close monitoring of the birds, to ensure their well-being, may cause added stress, though. Novices may become concerned by the fact that droppings become larger, looser and smell more strongly, and that the vent of the hen swells visibly. Be assured that this is perfectly natural and does not indicate that something is wrong.

EGG-LAYING

Once the hen is ready to lay she will produce eggs at daily intervals, although she may not begin to incubate them immediately. This should not be cause for alarm. It is common for incubation to begin only after two or three eggs have been laid, and there is good reason for this. If hatching takes place over several days, the young emerging later will be at a disadvantage when competing with their older, larger siblings for food. The chances of successfully raising a large clutch are much better when the young are all of similar size.

With canaries, it is normal practice to remove the eggs as they are laid and replace them with dummies. They should be kept at a steady ambient temperature similar to the cage from which they have been removed and out of draughts. Some breeders recommend turning the eggs a few times a day. Only after the full complement has been laid – generally about four eggs – are the eggs returned to the nest for incubation.

Although the birds should not be disturbed when they are laying, it is nevertheless important that they be carefully monitored. Occasionally an egg will become stuck in the lower section of the hen's reproductive tract, a condition known as egg-binding (see p80). This is a grave condition, potentially lethal, but can be treated by a vet provided there is no delay.

THE EGGS

It is often desirable to determine which eggs are fertile. If the eggs are uniformly white, as in the eggs of parrots, inspection is quite easy. Observing a high level of hygiene and cleanliness to prevent the spread of disease, the egg can be candled – that is, held up to a small, bright light source. While infertile eggs will appear uniform, those that contain developing embryos will show a distinct opacity, which increases with each passing day. For this reason eggs should be examined eight to 10 days after being laid. When eggs are not uniformly white, inspection is more difficult, as opacity is obscured by markings.

If a clutch proves infertile and the eggs are removed, the hen can be encouraged to mate again soon afterwards. The eggs should only be done removed if the birds are completely domesticated, though, as the disturbance to less robust individuals can disrupt the entire breeding season.

ABOVE *Canary eggs. Eggs that contain embryos show a distinct opacity, which increases every day.*
ABOVE LEFT *A canary in her well made nest, sitting on eggs.*

LEFT *Quails' eggs – a delicacy on restaurant menus.*

ABOVE AND ABOVE RIGHT
Canaries take around 15–17
days to fledge, growing a com-
plete set of feathers in that time.
BELOW *Young hand-reared*
Conures.

HATCHING

As the time for hatching approaches, the parent birds should be offered small quantities of the food required for rearing their chicks (see p67). The nest should not be disturbed unnecessarily to see if hatching has, indeed, occurred.

For some time after hatching, the young birds will not require feeding as they still have the remains of the yolk sac for nourishment. Gradually, though, both the volume and the composition of the food must be tailored to the needs of the growing family. The parents often display marked changes in their nutritional needs, too. Many finches and seed-eating softbills, for example, become ardent insectivores and, if deprived of this additional nourishment, may push their young from the nest.

OVERFEEDING

Strangely, it is overfeeding that can result in unexpected and particularly distressing behaviour in some parent birds. This is the tendency to eat their own young, a habit found particularly (but uncommonly) in corvids and Laughingthrushes. It is thought that the birds cannot distinguish their offspring from other live food. To avoid this, make live food harder to obtain; the parents will then have to forage away from the nest.

ARTIFICIAL INCUBATION

Parrot enthusiasts often resort to artificial incubation with the aim of raising survival rates of the young. The principal features of an incubator for this purpose are accurate temperature control (37°C; 99°F), humidity control and a means of turning the eggs externally.

Chicks that have been artificially incubated should be transferred to a thermostatically controlled brooder soon after hatching. The first feed is given about four hours after hatching, and usually consists of a special probiotic mixture designed to build up the necessary gut flora. Subsequent feeds, at roughly two-hour intervals, consist of specially formulated mixtures available from pet stores. The precise timing depends upon the time needed for the contents of the crop to pass through to the gut, and can be determined by touch. You should always be alert to the possibility of a blockage in the digestive tract, when the crop does not empty in the normal way. Immediate veterinary assistance should be sought as this condition may require surgery.

The serious breeder will have a pair of scales, accurate to a tenth of a gram, to monitor the growth of his or her charges. Maintaining a steady growth rate is important and can best be done by charting the growth for each chick on a graph.

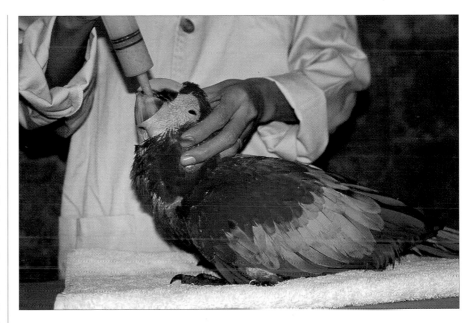

The interval between feeds can gradually be increased to four hours (for the larger species it may take three months of constant attention to bring a chick to fledgling). At this point a significant drop in weight may occur. Under normal circumstances the fledglings would now be preparing to leave the nest, so hand-reared youngsters must be provided with cages in which they can perch and stretch their wings. They must also be weaned from hand-feeding and allowed to feed themselves. The food, placed on the floor of the cage, is liable to become soiled quickly and must be constantly replaced in clean containers.

ABOVE *Hand-feeding a young macaw.*
BELOW LEFT *A baby Bali Starling* (Leucopsar rothschildi) *in an incubator, snug in a towel nest.*
BELOW RIGHT *Young Eclectus Parrots* (Eclectus roratus) *in a brooder.*

HAND-REARING

If possible, chicks should be hand-raised in groups rather than separately. Lone birds become strongly imprinted on their keepers and are harder to wean. However, such birds also make the best pets. If, as is to be hoped, the aim is to breed future generations, then young birds should be sexed early and allowed to form pair bonds at an early age as this greatly increases the chances for successful matings later in life.

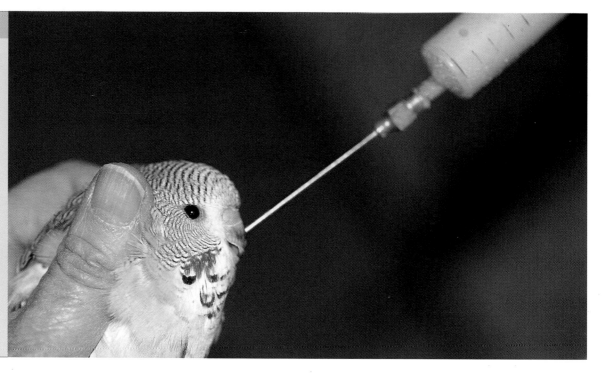

FOSTERING

Although many breeders are opposed to the use of foster parents, there are occasions when it is unavoidable, for example, if the hen dies. It is also useful with birds such as budgerigars that have a habit of eating their eggs, or with cockatiels that pluck the feathers from their young.

Some breeders resort to fostering for what can only be regarded as economic reasons – the more valuable birds being allowed to continue reproducing whilst the less valuable foster parents do the rearing. This happens particularly with Australian finches such as the Gouldian Finch, which is frequently raised by Bengalese Finches. It is, of course, important that the foster parents be reliable feeders and care properly for their adoptive brood. The number of fostered eggs should not exceed four, although they need not all be of the same species – just the same age requiring the same conditions for rearing.

The chief objection to fostering, apart from using the true parents simply as egg-laying machines, is that the fostered young come to identify themselves with the adoptive species, which can lead to reduced mating success in later life.

RECORD KEEPING

A major component of any successful breeding programme is proper record keeping. Today there are comprehensive database computer programs specifically designed for this purpose. Two of the best, Birdstud and Aviary Manager, can be downloaded from the Internet for a free trial period (www. petrie.starway.net.au/%7ewinners and www.aviary-manager.com.au). They allow for full record keeping on any number of bird species and individuals, providing information on call matings, family trees, feeding and medical histories. The programs also allow for sales and purchase records and all costs.

LEFT *When a bird is hand-reared, the first feed is given about four hours after hatching. Subsequent feeds are at two-hour intervals, gradually increasing to four.*

VIDEO OBSERVATION OF YOUR BIRDS

The development of miniature video surveillance equipment has now reached a point where it is a practical proposition for the bird-keeper. The systems are easily available, and affordable by anyone who values their birds and wishes to learn more about their habits and monitor their progress, particularly during breeding.

There are many advantages in monitoring aviaries, bird rooms and birds. One such advantage is security, if you suspect that theft may be a possibility. Monitoring may also cut short any disturbances by neighbours' pets or even wild animals straying near an aviary; disturbances may cause the birds to panic or even change their behaviour, with possible dire consequences. Then there are the mysterious happenings within the nest box. Until now, many a bird-keeper has queried why their breeding success is poor or nonexistent. Covert video surveillance can show whether or not eggs are laid or whether a rogue individual is destroying or eating eggs or young. The presence of anyone near the birds is usually enough to make them wary, so distracting them from malicious behaviour. This makes direct observation impractical, as you won't witness the culprit, so covert video surveillance is the only viable alternative.

Bird-watching by video camera is not only useful; the pleasure received by viewing birds, close-up, without their knowledge is well worth the cost.

CAMERAS AND LIGHTS

The simplest type of camera requires daylight for illumination of the subject; depending on the type of camera, pictures can be black or white, or colour. Understandably, colour systems are a little more sophisticated, and hence a little more expensive, but these are ideal for general observation within an aviary or a brightly lit bird room. Many colour video cameras incorporate a small microphone, so you can hear the sounds of your birds. These sensitive microphones cannot be waterproofed, so it is difficult to manufacture a totally watertight system catering for both video and sound. Nevertheless, these cameras are generally 'splash-proof', but do need to be positioned sensibly to avoid excessive moisture.

Nest boxes pose a different set of problems for video observation, as the inside of the nest box is usually illuminated by light coming through the entrance aperture only. Supplementary lighting must be provided, but be sure that it does not create any unnatural disturbance to the occupants. This really leaves only one possibility: infra-red; this light source creates neither heat nor light in the visual spectrum. However, the pictures will be seen as black and white only on the monitor screen.

You should be able to find a video camera that's reasonably small but also incorporates the infra-red light source within the same housing; some such cameras are totally waterproof, allowing their use in open aviaries, but these seldom incorporate a microphone. Most cameras are provided with a mounting bracket and instructions for fitting.

SAFETY

Video surveillance equipment is usually operated at low voltage, for safety reasons, but any cabling running outside permanent buildings should be well protected against the ravages of inclement weather, attacks by pests and even the birds themselves. Parrotlike birds, for instance, are notorious 'chewers', and would soon put the equipment out of action. Protect the cabling with a metal conduit and place a casing around any exposed camera parts; it is also useful to mount the nest box on the aviary or cage wall and allow the camera or cabling to protrude through the mounting surface of the box; this way it's inaccessible to the birds.

Any external cables should carry low voltage, and any power converter should be remotely fitted to comply with local electrical supply regulations.

SETTING UP A CLOSED CIRCUIT TELEVISION SYSTEM

Once you've decided on colour or monochrome, you need to choose a suitable monitor.

For most bird-keeper's purposes, a standard modern television set is ideal, as these can accept the camera's video signal through a standard in-built SCART

connector. (A SCART connector is a physical and electrical interconnection between two pieces of audio-visual equipment, such as a TV set and a VCR. Each device has a female 21-pin connector interface. SCART is an acronym for Syndicat francais des Constructeurs d'Appareils Radio et Television.)

ABOVE LEFT, ABOVE AND LEFT *Blue Tit in a nest box under surveillance. This is a delightful way to learn more about bird behaviour and discover insights into the mysteries of the nest box.*
OPPOSITE TOP *A miniature waterproof video camera and mounting brackets. Most cameras are at least splashproof, but few microphones are waterproof.*

The picture can then be viewed through the AV (Audio-visual) channel. Where a SCART input is unavailable on the television, it is still possible to convert the camera's video signal by means of a TV modulator unit so that a suitable RF (Radio Frequency) signal can be fed to the TV aerial socket.

You may prefer to use a video monitor; there are many good makes on the market, in black and white or colour, such as those used for security video surveillance. They normally accept a video signal only and cannot be tuned to receive RF television signals. This is usually the best method when a fixed system is required, such as the monitoring of an individual nest box.

Some situations may require more than one camera, or several cameras placed in different aviaries. To reduce the expense of multiple monitors, it is possible to feed each camera's video signal through a video switcher to display the images on a common monitor screen. Many types of switcher are available, giving different switching modes.

It is possible to divide the viewing screen into quarters with, for example, each quarter showing the image from one of four individual cameras simultaneously. Alternatively, the screen can show the image of each camera in turn This switching is achieved manually or by an automatically timed electronic switch.

Just like TV programmes, the signal from the video camera can be fed into a video recorder to record events when you are not present. And getting more sophisticated still, Time Lapse Recorders are available, which effectively slow down the passage of the video tape so extending the recording time. The image may not be as good as real-time video, but it is a way of capturing events that may otherwise be missed.

Putting together a video surveillance system will require time and thought, but it will be time well spent.

The possibilities are enormous, and it is usually wise to discuss the availability of components with a local security company or one of the larger pet and avicultural suppliers. The Internet is also a good resource for finding further information and suppliers.

INDEX

BIBLIOGRAPHY

Birds of Australia Jim Flegg and N Longmore (New Holland)
Birds of Australia P Rowland (New Holland/Struik)
Birds of Borneo GWH Davison and Chew Yen Fook (New Holland/Struik)
Birds of China and Hong Kong John MacKinnon and Nigel Hicks (New Holland/Struik)
Birds of East Africa Dave Richards (New Holland/Struik)
Birds of India and Nepal B Grewal (New Holland/Struik)
Birds of Java, Sumatra and Bali Tony Tilford (New Holland)
Birds of Namibia Ian Sinclair *et al* (New Holland/Struik)
Birds of Peninsular Malaysia and Singapore GWH Davison and Chew Yen Fook (New Holland)
Birds of South-East Asia Craig Robson (New Holland)

Birds of Thailand Michael Webster and Chew Yen Fook (New Holland)
Birds of the Himalayas Bikram Grewal and Otto Pfister (New Holland)
Crows and Jays Steve Madge *et al* (Houghton Mifflin)
The Distribution and Taxonomy of Birds of the World Charles Sibley *et al* (Yale University Press)
Finches and Sparrows Peter Clement *et al* (Princeton University Press)
Southern African Birds Ian Sinclair (New Holland/Struik)
Starlings and Mynas Chris Feare *et al* (Princeton University Press)
The Tanagers Morton and Phyllis Isler (Princeton University Press)
The Birdcare Handbook and Resource Guide (Seacoast Publishing)
The Complete Guide to the Roller Canary (Midland Roller Canary Club)
The Handbook of Birds of the World Del Hoyo *et al* (Lynx)

PHOTOGRAPH CREDITS

All photographs in this book were taken by the author, Tony Tilford, except for those in the following list.

Cooke, John (TC Nature) pp 8–9, 10 below left; 18–19; 27 top; 29; 30–31, 63 below; 75 below; 84–85; 135 top and below; 137
Froneman, Albert: pp 15 top right; 69
Hes, Lex (SIL): front cover (below left); back cover (top left); back cover flap (below)
Mangold, Walter: pp 79 below; 80 left and right; 81 top right; 82 top and below
Szymanowski, Janek (SIL): endpapers; pp 1–3; 6–7; 20–21 top right; 32 below left; 32–33 top right; 36–37; 38 top and below left; 42; 50 top and below right; 51 below left; 54–55; 62 top left; 70–71; 72 top left and top right; 74 top left; 79 top; 83 centre left and below; 98–99; 118 top and below; 122–123; 127 below left; 132 top left and top right; 133 below right; 134 below left
Thiel, Erhardt (SIL): p 14 below left
Von Horsten, Hein (SIL): dust jacket front flap